Praise for *The Lion's Den*

Good fiction mirrors life with a keen insight into the complexities of human existence. Great fiction inspires us to accept the terms of that bargain and relish the fleeting joys life has to offer us. In the case of Jerry Fabyanic's *The Lion's Den,* a sequel of sorts to his remarkable first effort, *Sisyphus Wins,* we experience not only the depths of human sorrow in living a life unfulfilled, but also the possibility that lies beyond. Focusing on the spiritual and personal evolution of Daniel, a Jesuit struggling with the repression of his own sexual identity, the story speaks also to a universal truth of questioning and finding oneself in the midst of a chaotic world with few intelligible answers.

Just as Fabyanic guides us through Daniel's quest to find himself in the midst of uncertain relationships both in himself and with others, he masterfully interweaves the story of Rafael and Miguel, allowing each of these threads to meaningfully inform the other. Brothers who were once students of Daniel, they now find themselves on the precipice of a fate they seem incapable of escaping. Haunted by the demons of their own tortured childhood, both follow a path of self-destruction, searching to make peace with themselves before it is too late. In the end, it is a story of love and forgiveness, of turmoil and survival, of loss and sacrifice in a life where sometimes even that is not quite enough. While *The Lion's Den* pushes the boundaries of our own self-definition, in the end it does so with what every great novel does: hope.

— Steven Craig,
High School English teacher
and Author of *Waiting for Today*

Jerry Fabyanic has produced a work that is both sensitive and powerful, centering on the lives, thoughts, and feelings of the protagonist and his circle of intriguing friends. We come to know a complex man whose complexities become increasingly evident as the story progresses. We feel with him as he reassesses his life and grapples with issues and emotions exploding around him. This journey, while unique to this group of people, has universal relevance.

There is another sort of universality here. The story has deep roots in philosophy, psychology (particularly Jungian), faith, and mysticism. These core concepts are developed through and intertwined with the characters and story. They are not given as a classroom lecture.

In short, *The Lion's Den* is a page-turner with meaning.

— John R. Taylor,
Retired Director of Investment and
Biotechnology/Healthcare Specialist

With the canyons and sage prairies of New Mexico and the foothills and mountains of Colorado as background, Jerry Fabyanic masterfully explores the story of Daniel, a conflicted Jesuit priest questioning his faith, relationships, and way forward. Like the character Jonathan, Jerry's focus is on what is hidden behind, beyond, or below the surface. Settings, such a room with morning shadows or the spiritual landscape of Chaco Canyon, often reflect the mood of the characters and create a sense of being there. Vivid dreams and riveting conversations take us into Daniel's world and the many motifs and archetypal themes interwoven throughout provide structure and a unique vision.

I found the book to be a page-turner, and I wanted to know what happens to the characters. *The Lion's Den* is an excellent portrayal of one man's journey. To be continued.

— Donna Taylor,
Former Human Resources Analyst
at an International Organization

With *The Lion's Den,* Jerry Fabyanic has crafted an immensely readable novel about real, fallible people who face and deal with the difficult issues of living. Daniel Patrick Murphy is an Everyman at a crucial time in his life. He is not only exploring his own self and motivations but also reaching out to others whose lives he has touched. Jerry's story is one to which the reader will relate, and they may find their own lives reflected in the sympathetic characters. One will find that the people and the story will stay in their mind well after the book has been completed.

— Marty McCune,
Retired Teacher and
Prolific Consumer of Great Literature

Jerry Fabyanic is a prolific writer who is a master at character development. In *The Lion's Den,* the reader easily perceives the feelings of Daniel as he grapples with his beliefs and the honesty of his relationships. Insightful Jonathan serves as the mainstay who imparts unshakable genuineness that counterbalances Daniel's unsettled desires. Jerry nudges us to determine if we will hold ourselves captive in the lion's den of life or break the bondage of the trappings of our minds.

— Judith Janson, M.S.
Retired I.B. Science teacher

THE LION'S DEN

BOOK TWO IN THE SISYPHUS SERIES

Also by Jerry Fabyanic

Sisyphus Wins

Food for Thought: Essays on Mind and Spirit: Volume One

Food for Thought: Essays on Mind and Spirit: Volume Two

The Lion's Den

Book Two in the Sisyphus Series

Jerry Fabyanic

Georgetown, CO 80444

The Lion's Den
Jerry Fabyanic

Published by Western Exposure

Georgetown, CO 80444
www.JerryFabyanic.com

ISBN: 978-0-9969636-5-7
LCCN: 2023910533

Editing by Melanie Mulhall, Dragonheart, TheDragonheart.com
Cover and interior design by Nick Zelinger, NZ Graphics, NZGraphics.com

First Edition
Printed in the United States of America

Author's Note

Despite the subtitle, "Book Two in the Sisyphus Series," *The Lion's Den* is not a true sequel to *Sisyphus Wins,* the first book in the series. Although reading *Sisyphus Wins* provides a deeper understanding of the relationship between the primary characters, Daniel and Jonathan, *The Lion's Den* can be read as a stand-alone work. Whether you choose to read either or both, I am thrilled and grateful that you are. My thanks.

"Then the king commanded, and they brought Daniel, and cast him into the den of the lions. Now the king spake and said unto Daniel, Thy God whom thou servest continually, he will deliver thee."

~ Daniel 6:16 (KJV)

1

THE VIBRANT ACADEMIC tenor of San Ignacio Academy and its curriculum mirrored the fertile verdancy of its surroundings but was a constant source of mental sepsis for the traditionalist archbishop of Denver. The campus was snugly nestled in the semiarid red rock terrain of the Colorado Rocky Mountain foothills, but its lush greenery belied the native environment over which it spread.

Seven brick buildings with terracotta tile roofs sat on the high points of the hilly terrain. Four of the buildings housed classrooms and labs, one a library and gymnasium, another the administrative offices, and the last a residence for the teaching staff. Each building's main entrance faced east and was illuminated by the morning sun's rays as students wended their ways to early classes. Each also had a west facing veranda that provided venues for students and faculty to intermingle, study, and discourse in the magnificence of God's creation. A glass roofed atrium provided indoor space in the center of the library and gymnasium complex for times of inclement weather.

The school was run by Jesuits, which afforded the teachers, those of the order and lay alike, the independence and space to work their craft liberally and expansively. Only a few decades old, the artfully designed campus had been created to emphasize the classical roots of learning that reached back long before the school's teaching order was founded by Ignatius of Loyola.

Students were to be taught not indoctrinated. Its mission, the school proclaimed, was to open the mind to allow the grace of God to enter not with a torrent or flood but by trickles, seepage, and gradation so that upon graduation, students would be prepared to live bounteous lives armed with a sound, rounded education. It was a precept of the school that faith based and promulgated on insubstantial belief was shallow and mundane, unable to withstand withering assault from reason. And the students thrived despite grousing by some about toiling under the demanding, rigorous expectations.

The expansiveness of the curriculum, which reflected the terrain on which the school nestled, rankled the archbishop. In his judgment, it was far too secular and deviated from Church doctrine and precept, and it flew in the face of his efforts to restore the Church to her earlier days.

It was within this swirling vortex of learning that Father Daniel Patrick Murphy had steered his crews of young minds for three decades. His disciplines included literature, writing, and philosophy, but he ventured into and engaged himself in related areas including art and psychology, blending them into his lessons. More than once he stirred up a hornet's nest of controversy, but he toiled on, buttressed by strong administrators and unwavering support from his students and their parents. When under undue pressure or in moments of crisis, he found strength in the Rubens painting *Daniel in the Lions' Den*, a copy of which hung on the wall behind his office desk, dominating the space. He would occasionally smile at the irony of finding personal power in the painting. Paul Rubens was a devout Catholic, and Father Daniel Patrick Murphy knew that this typification was not how some in the Church hierarchy saw him and his like-minded peers. In fact, he suspected those antagonists would prefer to see Catholics like him excommunicated.

Father Daniel glanced over at the papers he had brought with him to his private room, vestiges of the school year that had recently ended, and sighed. A chill ran down his spine. The usual seasonal dry heat had taken a sabbatical from the campus. The cold dampness of a lingering monsoon had refused to let up, and he struggled to breathe through his congested nasal passages. Pulling the wool afghan tighter, he coughed, first slightly and then more forcefully. The congestion refused to shake its grip. He reached for a tissue and looked over at Jonathan, who had been absorbed in his book.

Perhaps sensing Daniel staring at him, Jonathan leaned forward in his chair. "Can I make you more tea?"

Daniel smiled weakly. "Thank you. That would be lovely."

As Jonathan busied himself with the task, Daniel stared out the window at the wet gloom. The pelting rain reminded him of the cold, desolate feeling that had descended upon everyone still on campus. Not one to believe nature reflected human events, that pathetic delusion he insisted his students not include in their creative writing, he shook his head to clear his mind of the nonsense. Still, something was amiss. His gut, not the ceaseless rain that fell mercilessly over the Front Range of the Rocky Mountains, told him that.

He turned his attention back to Jonathan and watched him add honey and squeeze juice from a lemon slice into the mug as the water boiled noisily. Jonathan poured the water over the mixture and set the brew on the table between their chairs.

"Thank you," Daniel croaked in a whisper. He blew on the steam before he sipped. "How's the book?"

"Excellent. Again. *To a God Unknown* is one of my favorites to reread from time to time."

"How long ago did you last read it?" he asked hoarsely.

"A few years. When I was getting ready for my Joseph Campbell discussion group a couple of weeks ago, I read that in his young adult life, he and John Steinbeck were close friends. I hadn't known that. Apparently, they shared a common interest in mythology and were intrigued with Carl Jung's work and teachings on the collective unconscious. Interestingly, it was during that time, in the early 1930s, that Steinbeck began working on *To a God Unknown.* It took him five years to finish, even though it's a relatively short work when compared to *Grapes of Wrath* and *East of Eden.* I decided to do a fast read in prep for our discussion, but I couldn't do a fast read. Not with Steinbeck. I'm always captivated by his use of language."

"I always put Campbell within the context of his perspective on the quest for the Holy Grail, but right now, this doesn't feel much like a quest for the grail," Daniel replied.

"No, probably not. But it's part of the ordeal. Challenges to the hero aren't only clashing swords. They sometimes come as personal physical limitations or disabilities. Sometimes you have to smite while feeling crappy and being smote."

Daniel rocked a bit, forced another weak smile, and sipped his tea as he tried to focus on what Jonathan was saying.

"When I began reading Steinbeck and discovered Campbell, I didn't know of their friendship and common interests," Jonathan added. "But in hindsight, why they both have appealed to me makes sense. They both employ symbolism to explain self-realization and the conjunction of opposites."

Jonathan paused and stared out the window as if in thought and continued. "The myth of Cain and Abel has resonated with me since I first heard it, probably in the first grade. As a kid, it didn't make sense in lots of ways. I always thought Cain got the short end of the stick. It was obvious in my mind that Abel was Adam and Eve's favorite son. And having an older brother who was my mother's golden boy, I related to Cain. I felt sorry for him.

"When I began studying mythology and psychology, that twin motif took on a deeper meaning: Castor and Pollux. Romulus and Remus. Brother against brother. Jealousy. Betrayal. Delusion. Death to one. Since time immemorial, it's been a theme infused in stories of cultures worldwide. Steinbeck nails it in *East of Eden* with Cal and Aron. I consider it to be Steinbeck's opus, not *Grapes of Wrath*."

A rap on the door interrupted the conversation. The door opened slightly and a male voice asked from behind it, "May I come in?"

Daniel's face lit up and the pallid flesh gained some color, even if momentarily. "Vincente. What a wonderful surprise. Yes, come in, but I have to warn you, I'm fighting a cold that just won't go away."

Vincente nodded, giving the impression that he already knew.

Jonathan beamed, stood, and reached for Vincente's hand. "Brother Diaz-Romero, it has been ages."

"It has been, Jonathan. And remember, I'm no longer a Jesuit, so it's simply Vincente. You look well. How's it going?"

"I'm well, feeling well, and it's going well for me." He looked down at Daniel. "But not so well for our friend here, I'm afraid."

Vincente chuckled as he looked down at Daniel. "I guess I could comment about going to the well once too often, but I won't."

Daniel shook his head and groaned. "And I guess you couldn't leave well enough alone."

All three laughed.

"Your timing, Vincente, is fortuitous and timely," Jonathan said. "I need to head back up into the mountains. I have a few tasks to tend to, and I'm sure the highway has gotten dicey with this moisture. If it's rainy and chilly down here, you can be sure it's late spring snow in the high country." He turned toward Daniel. "I'll call you this evening, but don't hesitate to call if you need anything." Then he bowed slightly and said, "Namaste."

"Vincente," Jonathan said as he pulled on his jacket, "we do need to get together and catch up. I want to hear all about your new practice in New Mexico and what and who else is in your life."

Vincente gave Jonathan a hug. "A deal," he said. "I'd love to rendezvous. Better in New Mexico than up here. You know, it's much warmer and dryer down there."

"I sure hope so," Jonathan replied from the open doorway. "You have my number, so pick a place and text me. I'll pack my sandals and shorts and cruise south as soon as you give the word."

Once Jonathan pulled the door shut behind him, Vincente stepped over to Daniel and set a hand on Daniel's shoulder. "Tough going of late, eh?"

Daniel nodded and mouthed, "Yes."

"Let me brew a cup of tea before we start." He shivered a bit. "I can understand why you can't shake your cold. It rained nearly the whole way since I crossed into Colorado. I'm chilled to the bone."

As Vincente brewed his tea, Daniel pulled out the envelope with a draft of a letter he'd composed. He fiddled with the envelope as Vincente slid the chair Jonathan had been sitting on directly in front of Daniel and settled back into it.

"Start from the beginning," Vincente said, "and pull no punches. No secrets between us."

Daniel spoke about how everything was falling apart and how, for some reason, he felt worse was to come. "I feel like I am dying. I feel my life force ebbing away."

He talked about how he'd lost his sense of purpose and of how his relationship with Jonathan was mysteriously vaporizing and edging toward a breaking point. What compounded his feelings of guilt, he said, was that it seemed Jonathan was in denial, not picking up on the signs. Or maybe he was resisting. Daniel wasn't sure.

"Have you and Jonathan talked about it?" Vincente asked.

"Not in an in-depth way," Daniel replied. "We keep skirting around it."

Daniel fell silent and sipped his tea, rocking slowly. After a few moments, he spoke again. "I'm considering renouncing my vows and leaving the Jesuits as you did." He held up the envelope. "I've drafted a letter to be sent to my superiors, the archbishop, and the Pope asking them to dispense with my vows and laicize me."

Vincente nodded. "Have you lost your faith?"

"Faith? What is faith?" Daniel replied forcefully. "I'm not sure if I have faith to lose and wonder if I ever did. I certainly had beliefs. And I still believe. I believe in a God of some sort, but I'm finding it harder and harder to believe in the God of the Nicene Creed who's a father almighty, a man to the umpteenth power. Maybe I'm starting to believe in that God Unknown Jonathan has an affinity for, an ineffable, unknowable, ultimate energy. But faith?"

He paused and sipped his tea as Vincente remained attentive. "I once believed in the holy Roman Catholic Church, but I'm afraid I may no longer believe in it. At another time, we can compare notes on that, but in good faith, I feel I can no longer continue living a lie."

At the word *faith,* Vincente winced. "In good faith?" he asked. "Maybe there is an element of faith within you, but perhaps it is also a matter of semantics."

Daniel realized he'd used the word *faith* after just denying having any.

"May I see the letter?" Vincente asked.

Daniel passed it to him, and Vincente read without comment until he'd finished. "Short, concise, and to the point. It might take a while as it moves through the bureaucratic red tape, so be prepared to be in a holding pattern. I was only a brother, not a priest like you, which means more hoop jumping for you than my vow dispensation was for me."

Daniel nodded.

"You said you were *considering* leaving the order and priesthood, which indicates to me that you're not yet ready to toll the bell."

"I'm pretty much there, but as you know, this would be a weightier decision than entering in the first place. If I leave, there will be no turning back for me."

"No, there won't be."

"Once I make that decision, I will consider it final. And compounding my angst is a tempting offer of sorts from my aunt, who is my godmother. She and I have always been close. I'll tell you more about her at another time, but for now, let's just say that she was my support and mentor through my rough young adulthood."

"And her offer?"

"Again, details later, but it's lucrative and tempting."

"Have you mentioned this or talked it over at all with Jonathan?"

Daniel shook his head. "I'm afraid to because I think he'll not only encourage me, he will also expect us to follow up with a permanent, legal union. I don't want him to have unrealistic hopes. We've lingered in this nether world of commitments for years. He's been more than wonderful. Supportive in every way." He paused and looked earnestly at Vincente. "He deserves better. He deserves to know the truth. And he deserves someone better than me." Daniel paused again and offered an anemic smile. "I guess I just answered my own question."

A rap on the door interrupted their conversation.

"Father, I'm sorry to bother you," the housekeeper said through the door, "but there's a young man downstairs wanting to see you. He says his name is Stephen and that he is a friend of Miguel Rojas."

Daniel cast a quick glance to Vincente and raised his eyebrows. Vincente got up and cracked the door ajar. "Certainly, Maggie," Daniel said. "But forewarn him that I'm dealing with a nasty cold."

"Yes, of course, Father."

Daniel stood, folded the afghan, and brushed his fingers

through his hair. He looked at Vincente and gave a shrug. Vincente pulled the door open and stood silently, expressionless. A minute later, a fit young man who appeared to be in his twenties entered the room.

"Sorry to bother you on this not so pleasant evening, Father," he said. "My name is Stephen, and I wouldn't have intruded if it hadn't been important. Do you have a few minutes to talk to me?"

"Of course. Nice to meet you, Stephen. I understand this has something to do with Miguel Rojas. I hope nothing bad has happened. It's been quite some time—twelve years or more—since the Rojas twins were in my classes, but I remember them well."

The man glanced over at Vincente, who had stepped back and leaned against the bookcase with his arms folded. "Well, in all honesty, Father, it's not good. And this needs to be confidential."

"It's okay, Stephen," Daniel replied. "This is Vincente Diaz-Romero. He has my complete confidence."

The young man nodded. "Did you know Miguel well, Father?"

"I got to know both boys fairly well." He paused, not wanting to say more without knowing what Stephen's connection with Miguel was. "Pardon me for asking, Stephen, but what is your connection to Miguel?"

"Sorry, Father. I should have told you that up front." He looked down for a few seconds before raising his head and looking directly into Daniel's eyes. "I'm Miguel's boyfriend.

And I know quite a lot about his background: I know that his family were migrants and that they made their way from El Salvador through Mexico and entered Arizona across the Sonoran Desert."

Daniel nodded. "Yes, I believe two younger brothers died in the desert and an older sister was raped by the those who smuggled them and nearly died."

"Did you know that they came from an abusive situation, Father?" Stephen asked.

"Yes, I did. As I recall, their father had been a highly skilled carpenter in El Salvador. But when they were smuggled into the US, the whole family picked crops, first in New Mexico and then in Western Colorado, until they found their way to Summit County, where Miguel's father found work building apartments. I think the abuse started after the boys' mother died."

Stephen sighed deeply. "Yes, she'd found jobs cleaning and doing laundry for the big money people in their trophy homes." His voice carried a mixture of disdain and sadness. "But she got sick. And since they were illegal—or undocumented in today's jargon—the family turned to the Church and the immigrant community. And because she didn't get the treatment needed, she died. And that's when the abuse started. Miguel's father turned to the bottle. And the strap. And whatever else he could use to vent his rage on the boys."

"Yes," Daniel replied. "I know he used to beat the boys, especially Miguel, who stood up to him." Daniel had been so intent on what the young man was saying, he'd ignored the fact that the two were still standing close to the door. "Forgive me, Stephen. I'm not being at all hospitable. Please take a seat and tell me what this is all about. Would you like some tea?"

Daniel offered Stephen a seat and sank into his easy chair next to it.

"Thank you for the offer of tea, Father, but no. It's important that you understand the situation Miguel came from because it's relevant to what has happened."

Daniel leaned forward and connected with the young man's eyes. "And what exactly has happened, Stephen?"

"Well, I know that you counseled Miguel and Rafael at times. Is that the right word? Counseled?"

"Yes, that's an appropriate way of putting it," Daniel replied. "At the time, I taught religion, so we got into some pretty heavy stuff. It wasn't unusual for the discussions in class to veer into some pressing personal issues. They ended up in my classes because the parish priest arranged scholarships for them after they moved down to the Denver area. Their father had gotten a job but had lost it because of his drinking by that time. And their sister had met a guy and moved away after their mother died. So it was just the boys and their father."

Daniel coughed, picked up his tea, and took a few sips. When he put it down, he slipped a cough lozenge in his mouth.

"I'm sorry for coming at such a bad time. I can see you're not feeling well," Stephen said.

"Thank you. My cold seems entrenched. But let's not let that stop our conversation. You said this was important, and

I take that seriously." He paused before continuing. "Anyway, fortunately, the parish priest had seen potential in the boys."

He looked up at Stephen and smiled. "Miguel was the intellect. Brilliant. Surly, but brilliant. Rafael was an artist and poet. His work was filled with sadness and melancholy, but interestingly, not despair. Miguel, on the other hand, walked around as if there were a dark cloud hovering over him. His mind was a whirlwind. He sank into Nietzsche and Sartre. His was a dystopian world, dark and foreboding."

"For good reason," Stephen said strongly. "Their father became aware that they were gay, and that compounded the abuse." The look on his face told Daniel that even though Stephen appeared to be as much as ten years younger than Miguel, he'd already had his own experience with the mistreatment that often accompanied being gay.

"Father," he continued, "I know you counseled them and tried to help them."

"Well, I was primarily a compassionate listener," Daniel replied. "I knew that social services was involved but nothing changed. The boys' only hope seemed to be to survive until they could leave home. I met with each of them one-on-one at times, as I did with other students."

Daniel took another sip of tea. "But tell me, Stephen, what is this all about?"

"Sorry for taking so long to get to the point, Father. I just wanted to make sure I was doing the right thing in coming here." He took a deep breath and looked intently at Daniel.

"Miguel and I had … an argument that got violent. It happened in public. The police were called and Miguel was arrested."

"Good heavens," Daniel said quietly as he leaned forward in his seat. "Please continue."

"I was hurt badly enough to need medical attention, and when the police asked if I was willing to file a complaint, I felt I had no choice because this wasn't the first time Miguel had become … physical … with me, although he'd never really done harm in the past."

He paused and looked at Daniel beseechingly. "Father, I didn't want him to go to jail, but he needs help. When the DA talked with me, I begged her to not file charges against Miguel and explained Miguel's past. I didn't know what would happen, but after Miguel talked to the DA himself, he told me she'd offered to do something he called *defer prosecution* if he would agree to psychological help."

Daniel nodded. "And did he agree to it?"

"Yes, and he's been seeing a therapist, but the thing is, he's admitted to me that he doesn't really tell the therapist anything. And when he says anything to me about it, he mostly just says he can't talk to the therapist like he could talk to you."

Daniel sighed. "I admit that we had some pretty deep conversations about things like philosophy and religion, and he did reveal to me that he saw himself as being gay, which seemed to be one of the reasons his father was so hard on him. But when our sessions became increasingly personal and Miguel delved into the depth of darkness he felt within, I sensed I was in over my head. I'm not a psychologist, though I did have some training—enough, as we say, to get me into trouble. So I shared Miguel's story with Vincente, who was then the school's counselor."

Vincente stepped closer to Daniel. "Yes, Father Murphy and I were once colleagues. I've left the school, though, and I'm now laicized."

When Daniel saw that Stephen looked confused, he added, "That means he's left the Jesuits and is no longer a cleric of the Catholic Church."

"Yes," Vincente said, "I'm a psychologist in private practice now. In New Mexico, actually."

Stephen nodded at Vincente and then turned his attention back to Daniel. "Father, I'm sure you're wondering how all this involves you."

"Yes," Daniel admitted.

"I'm relieved that Miguel is seeing a psychologist. That means he's at least cooperating with the DA and probably won't be prosecuted, at least if he cooperates enough and sees it through. But what I've wanted all along since that … incident is for him to really be able to work through his issues."

He paused for a moment before continuing. "I know what that's like. I've had issues of my own, including some about being gay. And I know I look young, but let's just say I've done a lot of living so far, and I've had to at least begin to come to terms with my own stuff. I'd like that for Miguel too."

He again looked at Daniel beseechingly. "I'm wondering if you would be willing to help. To intervene with Miguel.

Maybe counsel him. I'm concerned that he might be suicidal. He'd still see his psychologist, but he'd also have sessions with you. I think he'd open up to you. More than once he's said he always felt comfortable talking to you."

Daniel furrowed his eyebrows. "Counsel him? Stephen, I'm no psychologist."

"I know, Father," Stephen replied. "But if you would be willing to meet with Miguel as you did when he was in school and encourage him, maybe you can pry him open a little. I think you may be the only one who could do that. I know I can't."

Daniel turned to Vincente and held his arms and hands out in supplication to indicate he needed help. Vincente took the cue.

"Stephen, forgive me, but can I help out here?"

Stephen nodded.

"Father Murphy has been under the weather for some time. As you can see, he's having a difficult time handling what you're saying because he's physically and mentally exhausted. He really isn't in a good position to agree to something of this nature. Do you need an answer right now? Could Father Murphy let you know after he's feeling better?"

"Of course. I realize that this would be a major commitment." He turned toward Daniel. "Father, I admit that I'm a bit desperate, but I think you could help. Miguel trusts you, and so do I. I know that you will make the right decision." He stood, reached into his jeans pocket, and pulled out a piece of paper. "Here's my cell phone number, Father. Please let me know when you've made your decision." He offered a weak smile. "Whatever it is."

Daniel nodded as he took the slip of paper and studied it. "I have just one question, Stephen. Is Miguel aware that you're here?"

"No, Father. But of course, if you agree to counsel him, I'll have to tell him about our conversation. Then it will be up to him to decide if he's willing to see you."

Daniel rose and accompanied Stephen to the door. "I'll pray on it. And I'll let you know. In fact, I'll pray for all of us."

Stephen raised his eyebrows, as if surprised. "Thank you, Father. I don't think anyone has ever prayed for me before … except for my parents and people in my church who tried to pray my gay away."

Daniel put an arm on his shoulder. "Stephen, I'll pray that you continue to be the beautiful and courageous soul you are."

2

FATHER DANIEL PATRICK Murphy stood at the window and stared out at the relentless gray drizzle and raindrops languidly making their way down the panes. He traced a few with his finger as a shiver ran down his spine. He closed the shade to block out the visual gloom, pulled his robe tighter, and glanced over at the remains of the chicken soup and grilled cheese sandwich Maggie had delivered on a tray for lunch. It had helped warm the chill that pervaded his body, but he hadn't much of an appetite.

He decided he needed something more potent. He pulled open the lower door of his cabinet and retrieved the bottle of Baileys and poured himself a snifter. Perhaps it would help distract his mind from the previous evening's conversation with Stephen. And Miguel. Between them, his cold, and the dreary conditions, his sleep had been fitful and minimal.

After settling in his easy chair, he took a sip of the Baileys and reached for the sketch pad on which he had written *Archetypes* in the center and circled it. At the top he had written *Soothsayer,* at the bottom *Chameleon,* on the left *Shapeshifter,* and on the right *Fabulist.* From each, he had drawn connecting lines to the circle. He stared at the schematic and mused. That's me, he thought.

He flipped the page to a blank sheet and stared at it wondering what to write or sketch. Then he checked himself as he realized he was forcing stuff. It was best, as he always told his students when doing an activity, to allow whatever came up to work its magic even if it seemed like dark magic. He shifted his weight, and out of the corner of his eye spotted his copy of Carl Jung's *Answer to Job* that lay face down on the lamp table. He vaguely recalled the excerpt about antinomy and picked up the book, scanning through it to find the passage, and reread Jung's words, which he'd highlighted. Yes, antinomy, he thought, as he wrote the word in large letters in the center of the page and drew a circle around it. A moment later, after only a brief reflection of it, he tore the page from the tablet, crumpled it, and tossed it toward the wastebasket next to his desk. It lay on the carpet scattered among dozens of other balled up wads.

He took another sip of the Baileys and squinted his eyes in thought. A light seemed to come on in his mind. He turned the pad ninety degrees for it to be in landscape layout and rewrote the word. *Antinomy.* This time he drew an oval around it. Better, he thought. Two-sided. Opposites of parallel but opposing truths. To the left and right of the oval, he printed his and Jonathan's names and drew circles around both names. Yes. The soul as a circle. Plato thought so.

At the bottom of the sheet in the center, Daniel printed *Us*, drew an oval around it, and connected it to the circled names with lines. He picked up *Answer to Job* and reread the passage. Yes, God was like his human creations: a totality of inner opposites and forever in conflict with himself. Above his name on the sketchpad, he printed *Omnipotent* and above Jonathan's name, he wrote *Omniscient.* Taking another sip, he stared at his creation, shook his head, and scratched out the circled names. He drew a line through *Us* and wrote *Me* and squiggled a line over the straight line he had connected the oval to Jonathan's soul circle.

"This is about me," he whispered, "not Jonathan."

After another sip of Baileys, he crossed out the prefix *Omni* from *Omnipotent* above his name and in its place printed *Im.* I am that, he thought. Impotent. He then drew a line through *Omniscient* and above it printed *Disingenuous.* Yes, he thought, impotent and disingenuous. Weak and untruthful. He lifted the snifter to his lips and inhaled the last of the Baileys before closing his pad.

Daniel's mind swirled in convolutions as he thought about his state of being. Dissolution. Things were falling apart. They had been for some time, slowly and incrementally at first but now increasing in tempo. Reaching a crescendo? Maybe. To describe his reluctance to communicate with those he loved and his closest friends and confidants—Jonathan, James, Richard—as disingenuous was in itself disingenuous. Evasive? Yes. But more. Worse. A lie of omission. He was not telling them the full truth, and it wasn't right. Especially with Jonathan. With him, it was deeply personal. True to his nature, though confused and undoubtedly struggling to make sense of what was happening, Jonathan remained true. He wouldn't quit. He stood steadfast with Daniel, deluding himself, Daniel believed, that when the pixie dust settled, all would be right.

Perhaps he's not omniscient after all, he thought.

It wasn't fair and was even cruel, but Daniel knew he could not bear carrying another cross—the one he would take on by being completely open with Jonathan. At least not yet. The immediate burden was the truth he had suppressed and sequestered in his shadow for years, which had risen to the surface of consciousness and needed to be confronted. But as painful as it was for them, Jonathan and their relationship would have to wait.

He sat down in his easy chair and pulled the afghan up around him. Everything would have to wait for a little while.

The tap on his door and Maggie's voice awakened him. "Father, will you be coming down for dinner?" she asked through the closed door.

He groggily reached for his phone to check the time. It was almost six. He'd slept for some time. "Thanks, Maggie," he replied. "I'll be down shortly."

Daniel laid his head back down and rubbed his head. It hurt. The Baileys helped him sleep, but it inflicted a painful aftereffect. He listened to the rain drumming steadily against the window. Shivering, Stephen's request flooded back to his mind. Miguel. He had seen him only that one time since graduation over a decade ago. He recalled liking Miguel as a student but also not being unhappy when he graduated. Miguel was a veritable human black hole sucking in every bit of energy from those around him and using it to feed his fire. And yet …

"Stop it!" he croaked. "Quit thinking of him!" Slowly sitting up, he noticed something. His sinuses, while not clear, were opening. He actually smelled something: tuna fish casserole. It was Maggie's Friday night special. She had probably made her secret recipe for spicy tomato soup to go with it.

He lifted himself up from his chair and made his way to the bath to wash up. The half-eaten chicken soup and grilled cheese sandwich derided him as he walked past them. They were like the weather and his mood, cold and dreary without a ray of hope.

After putting on a fresh shirt, he carried the lunch tray down to the kitchen and set it on the counter. He whispered a thank you to Maggie and made his way to the dining room where James and Richard sat engaged in quiet conversation. They stood when he walked in.

"Brother," they greeted him.

"Thank you, brothers," he said as they sat. "To say the least, these have not been among my better days."

Maggie came from the kitchen carrying a covered dish. "Tuna fish casserole. Extra warm. The soup is still hot, so don't wait," she added before scurrying out.

Daniel inhaled deeply, savoring the warming aromas wafting through the room. "Maybe Maggie's cooking is the cure for the cold," he said.

The two priests grinned, and Father Richard gave a hearty, "Hear! Hear!"

"It's a blessing to share this meal with my brothers," Father James said. "Let us join hands for grace."

"Considering my cold, it might be better to not touch my hand," Daniel replied.

"I imagine you washed thoroughly before coming down," Father James said. "We're not afraid."

Daniel nodded and took the others' outstretched hands.

Father James closed his eyes and intoned, "Heavenly Father, we thank you for our bounty. We thank you for bringing us together in the spirit of love and support. We ask you to bestow peace, guidance, and wisdom upon us as we continue your work in your earthly kingdom. Lord, we ask you to especially bless our brother Daniel during his challenging time. And help him understand that we, his brothers in Christ, are with him, love him, and will support him in whatever trials and tribulations he might encounter. Amen."

"Amen," said Father Richard.

Raising his head as they released their hands, Daniel looked at his two friends and said, "Thank you, brothers."

Father Richard began scooping casserole onto their plates as Father James ladled the soup into their bowls. He took a warm roll from the basket and passed the basket to Daniel. After their plates were filled, James raised his glass.

"This is not a toast, but a reminder of Jesus and his disciples sharing a cup of wine when they broke bread. Of course, they didn't have the benefit of Maggie's world-renowned tomato soup, tuna casserole, and dinner rolls, so perhaps we are more blessed than our Lord."

The three chuckled and clinked their glasses.

Daniel began buttering his roll. "Well, brothers," he said, "I had a visitor last night—besides Vincente—and I'd like to talk with you about the situation. A former student is in a bad place right now. He assaulted his boyfriend pretty badly, and he's getting psychological care as part of an agreement to avoid prosecution."

The two priests nodded in understanding and continued eating without interrupting.

"He's been resistant to intervention even though he agreed to it, and his friend—the boyfriend he assaulted—thinks that maybe I could pierce his bubble. So he would like me to agree to counseling him."

"How long ago was he your student?" James asked.

"About twelve years ago, but I'll check the records to be sure. His name is Miguel. His twin, Rafael, was also my student. Both were brilliant but in different ways. Miguel was the intellectual genius. Rafael, the artist. They came from a very troubled migrant family and were horribly abused by their father after their mother died."

"Do you think that trauma is behind this?" Richard asked.

"I have no doubt that it's at the root, but I'm sensing there's more. I ran into Miguel once after graduation. We chatted a bit, but I haven't seen him since, and I did see Rafael several years ago when he called on me during a visit to Denver. But that's another story."

"It's troubling, to be sure," James replied. "I feel for the lads. Have you decided on how to proceed?"

"No. Fortunately, Vincente rescued me. I told the boyfriend, Stephen, that I'd get back to him. But I'm not sure how soon. So much to unpack."

"I understand your quandary," Richard said. "On the one hand, we enjoy it when former students reconnect with us to let us know how they're doing. It's wonderful to know you impacted them enough for them to take the time to tell you. On the other hand, when they're troubled, it can be hard to hear about their struggles. It can put you in a bind because you feel you need to intervene, not just listen, even though they may only need a good ear and a caring hug."

"Several former students of mine have tragically died or been killed," James added. "Some in car accidents and others from health complications, some of which they'd dealt with from birth. The toughest, though, were the ones who died of drug overdose or suicide."

Richard nodded. "You're right about that, James. One young man's death particularly shook me. His name was Dean, and he was one of the brightest in a class filled with bright ones. Gentle spirit. Always a smile on his face. He went off to college, and during his senior year, he killed himself by sitting in his car with it idling in his closed garage. I was devastated, as was everyone else.

"After the celebration of his life his parents had for him, I got talking to his younger sister. She told me Dean dealt with mental health issues all his life. I was stunned. I not only hadn't been aware of it, I never suspected it. I asked her why her parents didn't let us know. She said they had been doing all the right stuff—therapy and medications—but they didn't want him to be treated differently, and neither did he. I think I understood their point, but then again, I was troubled by it.

I'm not sure if knowing about his condition would've helped, but I still wish I had known."

"It's a tough call," James said. "I can't imagine what a parent goes through when their child is dealing with mental health issues. They want the best for them, but they don't want them stigmatized. And in time, the young person has to make it on their own. The parent knows their child has special needs, but they also know their child has to become independent, at least in most cases."

"I agree," said Richard. "I didn't question Dean's parents' decision. Would it have helped him if I'd known? Arguably not. But it did make me really ponder the question. And it made me more conscious about other students. I never forgot the insight a fellow teacher gave me when I first got into the classroom. During our planning time, I was venting about one or more of my more challenging students. He listened empathetically, but when I finished, he said, 'If you knew what kind of homelife some of these kids have, you'd be surprised how well they behave here, how functional they are.' I never forgot that and have it in mind every time I sit with a troubled student to counsel them."

Daniel, who had sat taking in the exchange between his two peers, set his fork down and eased back in his chair. "Thank you, brothers. Everything you said has resonated. You've helped make clear in my mind what I need to do. I cannot imagine what a teacher must feel when they learn that one of their former students has committed a crime or committed suicide. And I understand there are troubled souls like Miguel who might come back into my life. In a way, it isn't surprising to hear of Miguel's struggles. What surprises me is that he speaks of me so highly." He shook his head. "Why me?"

"Why not you?" James asked. "It's obvious that for one reason or another, Miguel holds you in high esteem. You don't know why at this point, but as you know, there is only one way to find out."

Daniel sighed. "A few weeks ago, it might've been an easy call. A few years ago, an even easier one. But now, not so easy." He drained the rest of his wine. "But I guess we don't get to pick the best times for crises to show up on our doorstep. And sometimes they come one after another." He stood. "Thank you again, brothers. I know what I need to do, but first I need to get some sleep. That's been a rare commodity of late."

3

VINCENTE CHECKED THE time and saw he had plenty of it to get to the Bodhi Manda Zen Center in Jemez Springs where he would meet Jonathan. He figured it would be about a ninety-minute drive. Jonathan was doing a retreat in Chaco Canyon, and he had said it would take a few hours for him to drive from Chaco Canyon to the center, so Vincente had no need to rush. He glanced out the window and took a minute to soak in the beauty that surrounded him. It was a typical gorgeous Santa Fe day, the kind he never took for granted.

He put the novel he was reading down on his office desk and eased back into his chair. Taking a break at the office to read novels and stories of little-known or forgotten history had proven to be rejuvenating and stimulating. He picked up his cup of cappuccino and focused his attention on the three art pieces hanging on the wall across from his desk. They depicted scenes from the early Spanish conquest and settlement of the Southwest, a time when his family's ancestors settled in the New World. The novel was about the Sephardic Jews who had migrated to New Mexico during the Spanish Inquisition, and he wondered if there was a lineage in his family directly tied to them.

Musing about the possibility that he might be part Jewish, he thought of the families he knew that had done serious genealogical research and discovered they were descendants of the original Sephardic Jews. Could his family have that connection too? It would be an intriguing pursuit. He made a mental note to run it by Sophia and get her take. Being more curious than him, Vincente knew she would be all in.

Putting aside that intriguing possibility, Vincente refocused his attention on his old friend Daniel. When Daniel initially reached out and asked Vincente if he could make a quick trip up to Denver so he could talk over some stuff that was wracking him, he realized things were not good for Daniel. Some inner demons were upending his life, and the issue with Miguel was complicating stuff further.

Not only did he know Daniel well, Daniel was always completely honest with him. Vincente was the one person Daniel would bare his soul to. Even after all their years together, Jonathan was not privileged to completely peer into what lay in Daniel's heart.

Vincente sat back up and pulled up the initial email from Daniel on his computer. Even though Daniel attempted to be uplifting, the message between the lines strongly suggested something wasn't right. Now he was aware, at least in part, of the reasons for that being the case. But to have Daniel's email to be followed up by one from Jonathan, whom he had gotten to know only cursorily, confirmed his suspicion.

After they met again by happenstance in Daniel's room, Vincente knew he had to engage with Jonathan on a deeper level. But in their exchanges afterward, he too seemed cryptic. Their conversation, Jonathan said, would need to be private and in person: no phone and absolutely no emails or texts about the specifics of the issues. Both men were being guarded. Was it merely fortuitous for Jonathan to be with Daniel when Vincente arrived? Or was it synchronistic? Or did Jonathan know he was heading up to see Daniel?

Vincente finished his coffee and texted Sophia that he was heading off but would be back in time for the cocktail party they were invited to the next evening. But as he grabbed his bag on the way out the door, it occurred to him that this might be the perfect excuse for missing the party. An out-of-town emergency he had to take care of.

He laughed mischievously as he left the building. He hated snooty soirees at which uberwealthy magnates droned on about their magnificent but boring lives while decrying the problems of the world. It was one thing to listen to their angst in therapy sessions. It was another thing to be subjected to it at a social function. He slammed the tailgate shut after tossing in his bag and looked up at the blue sky. Life's good for me, he thought, but not for so many others. Vincente climbed up into the cab, fired up the engine, and headed out.

Less than ninety minutes later, he reached the Bodhi Manda Zen Center. It had been a warm, dry spring in the Jemez Valley. The pinyon pines, junipers, and sage were, nevertheless, rich in their greenery due to the ample snowfall that had blanketed the region earlier. The waters of the creek that flowed through the center property, fed by melting snow, splashed and crashed against the rocks that abounded in the creek bed. It was a place impervious to time. Its clean, crisp evening air served as an elixir for any troubled soul.

Vincente thought of that as he pulled into the center. As he climbed down from his truck, he breathed deeply, taking in the aroma of sage and pine wafting through the air. It was invigorating. He was thinking that it would be good if Daniel were here. It would be the perfect place to begin healing and renewing his body, mind, and spirit. He lifted his bag from the truck bed, pulled it over his shoulder, and looked up to see Jonathan coming up to meet him.

"Jonathan!" he said as they embraced.

"Vincente! It is so good to see you. Thank you for coming."

"Of course. It's been a while since I've been able to come here and detach from life. What a day, eh?"

"It is. No need to check in. I already got our room, and you're in time for dinner. I volunteered us for KP after dinner. I hope you're okay with that."

"More than happy to do KP," Vincente said as they made their way to the dorm area. "I love sinking my soft, over-washed hands into dishwater and scrubbing pots." He glanced around at the few vehicles in the lot and the relative quiet across the campus. "It's not looking too busy."

"No. Surprisingly, it's not. Looks like we've timed it perfectly. When I checked in earlier, a large group was checking out. I had to wait to get into the room, but it was okay. I used the time to do some *kinhin*."

"What's that?"

"Walking meditation." Jonathan pointed to a bunk bed as they entered the room. "That one is yours. Go ahead and freshen up, and I'll meet you in the dining hall."

"Sounds good. I'm looking forward to a nice soak in the hot springs pool afterward. It will be a good place to exchange thoughts and see if we can figure out what the hell is going on with our friend."

After finishing dinner and scrubbing the pots and pans, Vincente and Jonathan ambled back to their room. They walked quietly, taking in the darkening evening sky that was beginning to be populated by stars. Jonathan pointed to one particularly bright light in the sky.

"I think that's Venus," he said.

"Could be," Vincente replied. "I've never been able to identify with certainty which ones are stars and which ones are planets."

"Me neither, but I figure the brightest light in the evening sky must be Venus."

"Why?"

"I don't know. Maybe it's because she's the goddess of love."

"You realize the planet is a poisonous, gaseous glob."

"Yeah. Kind of romantic to think about, don't you think?"

Vincente looked sideways at Jonathan and caught Jonathan smiling.

"That's the irony of love," Jonathan said. "On the surface, it's wondrously beautiful to behold. But dive below the surface and you often find a swirling miasma of inimical energy that can do you in. I figure if two people can survive that, they have a chance."

Vincente stared at Jonathan for a moment. In return, Jonathan raised his eyebrows, widened his eyes, and smiled again.

"You're an enigma," Vincente said as they reached the door. "You go ahead. I need to text Sophia to let her know I'm fine."

Once Vincente had traded texts with Sophia, he got undressed, put on a pair of trunks and flipflops, wrapped himself in a white Turkish towel, and headed to the hot mineral springs pool. Jonathan was already there, and Vincente gazed down on him floating in the water. He thought about Jonathan's oblique musing comparing true love to the reality of Venus. A pang of guilt ran through him knowing he had told Jonathan less than half of the story when they spoke on the phone. He had told him about Miguel, but he hadn't shared the information about Daniel considering leaving the Jesuits, the priesthood, and worse, perhaps leaving him. His heart ached for both men, but it wasn't his role or right to tell Jonathan the rest.

"I like coming in May," Vincente said as he stepped into the pool. "Not too warm, which makes the pool much more embracing." Jonathan remained floating, and Vincente joined him, lying back and allowing himself to float. He splashed some water on his upper body and gazed up to the sky. "It's good to see you, Jonathan."

"Same here, Vincente. I wish it were under better circumstances. When this finally gets resolved, we'll need to do a real retreat. Not talk about problems but do some serious meditation and mindfulness practices."

"You're on. I'd love it."

Jonathan pulled himself into a seated position with his arms draped over the side of the pool. Vincente did likewise.

"About Daniel," Jonathan said. "I called him before I left to check on how he was feeling. He said he was beginning to feel much better, but it would likely still be a few more days before he got completely over it. I told him I was going to Chaco for a few days to do some walking meditation. He agreed it would be good for me and asked that I keep him in my intentions when I did my practices. I didn't mention I was meeting you, of course."

"I'm glad you called him. It's important for him to have a sense of normalcy."

Even through the rising mist, Vincente noticed the tears welling up in Jonathan's eyes and had heard the aching in his voice. "Jonathan, I wish I had the words to console you or explain it all, but I don't. Even though you might not feel it now, no one knows Daniel better than you. While you don't know the facts of this, you know the most important part of him—his soul."

Jonathan shook his head slightly. "I used to think that, but I'm not so sure now. Things have become less clear and more imbalanced. Despite considerable consternation, I reluctantly wrote it off to the staleness that can set in on any relationship.

I say reluctantly because my head told me that's all it is, but my gut keeps telling me otherwise."

"I can understand where you're coming from. When I began feeling uncomfortable about remaining with the Jesuits, I couldn't figure out why. Like you, I attributed it to mundane reasons like how I found being celibate repressive and how frustrated I felt with the rigidity of Catholicism. But after my interaction with Daniel and the Rojas boys, I saw through the fog. It helped me make sense of my anger about the harm the Church does in the name of tradition and institutional self-preservation. I saw it firsthand in very personal terms."

"It's tragic. I had my own epiphany about that long ago. Another time I'll tell you about the last time I was in a Catholic church."

"I'd love to hear about it."

Jonathan tightened his mouth and nodded.

Vincente continued when he said nothing further. "I can't clearly explain how or why Daniel and I became such close friends, but over time, I came to see him for what he truly is. He's something we rarely see the likes of today. He seems a contradiction, but he's not. Daniel is the most complex person I've ever known. At first glance, he comes across as serious and stern, which he can be, but within that shell lies a most caring, compassionate, gentle soul, a heart burning with unconditional paternalistic love, and a self-reflecting mind. He constantly challenges himself, sometimes to his detriment. When he does that, he can intellectually and emotionally turn himself into a pretzel.

"As the counselor for his students, I repeatedly heard first-person praise of him. Not one boy ever spoke of him harshly. Oh, they'd get angry with him when he refused to accept inferior, shoddy work, but once we talked it through, they invariably came around to being appreciative for what they were learning and the intellectual rigor he was instilling in them. One thing I never told him, which I now regret, is that almost every one of them said they knew he was gay and it didn't matter to them. Their testimonials continually blew me away."

"Was that true for Miguel?"

"It was. More so, even. On steroids. I think Miguel became infatuated with Daniel. He was possessive and jealous when Daniel gave another student more attention than him. Especially to his brother, Rafael."

"Did Daniel know that?"

"I don't think so, and by his reaction to the request that he intervene with Miguel, it seems he still doesn't." Vincente paused and looked off to the side. "But there was more. Something was happening to Miguel, with Miguel. Whenever I steered our conversations there, Miguel become evasive."

"And Daniel? He also suspected something not being quite right?"

"It's the reason he decided to no longer meet with Miguel one-on-one and turned him over to me."

Jonathan looked directly into Vincente's eyes. "Vincente, I know you're being as candid and honest with me as you can. But I sense there's more. There has to be."

Vincente stared back at Jonathan and then lowered his eyes to the water. He inhaled deeply before looking back up at Jonathan. "There is, but it's something you'll need to ask Daniel about. But wait until the time's right. Until then, I believe it would be good for you and me to keep talking. You're his partner. I am, or at least I used to be, his closest friend and confidant."

Jonathan nodded. "Thank you, Vincente. I need to set my issues aside and focus on helping Daniel. It's as if I'm riding atop a swirling maelstrom, and I feel it would suck me in and swallow me if I let it."

"I hear you. Like riding a wave, only the wave is not headed to a shore where it will crash on a beach but swirls in an endless spiral."

Jonathan bit his lower lip. "Yeah, and I dare not fall off. I can't swim." He tilted his head back and allowed his body to float again. Vincente did likewise, and both men stared up into the heavens taking in the stars misted over by the steam.

"I love staring into the night sky," Jonathan said. "It's mysterious and mesmerizing. Especially Venus."

"Like human relationships."

Jonathan looked over at Vincente. "Speaking of which, congratulations on yours. What's her name again? You said it earlier."

"Sophia."

"Ah, wisdom. God's consort. How did you meet her?"

"At a conference. It sounds like a teenage thing, but when

I watched her presentation, I just knew she was the one. She was and is."

"When do I get to meet her?"

"How about on your way back. Spend the night with us in Santa Fe. She'd love to get to know you." He paused and turned to Jonathan with a wink and a smile. "I will admit it would also be a little self-serving. An out-of-town friend showing up unexpectedly would give me the perfect out for skipping a cocktail party I've been dreading going to."

Jonathan smiled broadly in return. "I'd love it, and I'm pleased that I can be part of your nefarious scheme. Thank you, Vincente."

4

FATHER DANIEL STOOD in the center of his room and stretched his arms out wide. While he was pretty much over the cold physically, he was still mentally enervated. The good thing, he mused, was that he was no longer contagious. He closed his eyes and slowly turned counterclockwise. As he turned, he pictured his room with its the sand-colored walls and dark green carpeting. It was a safe place, his own little cubicle in the universe. Taking a deep breath, he inhaled the spice incense that he was now able to smell.

When he stopped and opened his eyes, in front of him was the dark mahogany door to his bath. It was ajar and his bathrobe hung next to it. To the left of his bath, his desk sat in a small workspace. He stepped over to a corner table that served as his tea stand, poured some boiling water into his mug, and steeped a cup of black chai. Then he set the hot brew on the small table next to his chair and eased himself down, closed his eyes, and rocked, allowing the creaking chair to massage the weariness that still pervaded his mind.

Daniel stared at the framed photograph of Delicate Arch hanging on a wall. It was one he had taken when he and Jonathan camped in Utah's Arches National Park years earlier.

The arch reflected the setting sun's soft rays but the sky behind it was a threatening heavy gray indicative of a storm in the distance. Contrasting images of light and dark had always mesmerized him, and that scene, at that precise moment in time, captured it perfectly.

He thought about that trip with Jonathan. He and Jonathan had recently met, and life with him was filled with promise. He closed his eyes and offered a prayer of gratitude for having had Jonathan in his life. Then he opened his eyes and scanned the room that had been his cell over the past two decades.

A thought drew his attention to the bookshelf that stood between two small casement windows. The unfolding of the day's events ate at him. His gut was telling him he would find answers not in prayer but in Jung, so he set his cup down and walked over to the bookshelf that held his library. He ran his finger across the spines of the well-worn books and stopped on Carl Jung's *Memories, Dreams, Reflections.* When he sat back down with it, he let the tome rest on his lap as he sipped more tea. His thoughts suddenly jumped to his old friend Jean Luc and a recent tragedy his friend had told him about. Jean Luc had coped with the tragedy and found a way to move forward from it after reading Robert Hopcke's book *There Are No Accidents*. The irony was that Jean Luc had forgotten that Daniel had given him the book. It showed that there are no accidents, he thought.

As he sipped his tea, Daniel mused about how Hopcke explored synchronicities in peoples' lives, including the synchronicity of two people having the same dream. It made sense to Daniel. In his mind, it was no different than how, according to quantum physics, one particle could be in two different places at the same time. Not being a physicist or even having the scientific acumen of one, Daniel accepted that prima facie. His decades in academia, rightly or wrongly, developed in him a faith and acceptance of findings produced by authorities in other disciplines whose research was rigorously peer vetted and tested. Nor was he a trained psychologist, but he had become comfortable in that discipline, given his extensive coursework in that field and his degrees in theology, biblical history, and literature.

As he reflected on Hopcke, his mind jumped back to Jung and *Memories, Dreams, Reflections.* He cradled the copy, which he had bookmarked and dogeared extensively, and rocked. Realizing he had no tea left when he lifted his cup to take another sip, he thought of brewing another cup but thought better of it. Despite the caffeine, chai had a relaxing effect on him, even this late in the evening, but one was enough. A cup of sage herbal would be better, he decided. For him, it was therapeutic.

As he stood waiting for the water to come to a boil, Daniel reflected on the unsettling dream that had put him out of sorts since he woke in a start in the predawn hours. It puzzled him, which made him wonder about its power. So despite his weariness, he knew he would not sleep until he gave it attention. From Daniel's perspective, Jung had a detached way of exploring and presenting problems regardless of how emotionally charged they were. And Jung shared at least one thing with Daniel: Dreams did not help either of them move past their disorientations.

Daniel thought about Jung's account of dreaming he was having a conversation with his father, who had died over two decades earlier. His father, who had not been a warm, loving husband or parent, was asking his son for marital advice. Jung considered the dream odd until his mother died soon after. Jung concluded his father was using the medium of the dream to ask for guidance about how to proceed with his soon-to-be-arriving wife. It would be a fresh start for them, so to speak.

Jung's discussion about Johann Wolfgang von Goethe's *Faust* also intrigued Daniel. Like Jung, Daniel considered the story a personal one. He, like Jung, saw within himself a conjunction of opposites. Daniel was beginning to sense that Mephistopheles, the devil, personified his shadow and was now animating his life. In a way, the thought of it was intoxicating, yet it was also discomforting.

After settling back in his chair with his fresh cup of tea, Daniel opened the book to the passage he'd bookmarked and highlighted. Jung had written about how Faust had struck a chord in him, piercing him in a deeply personal way. He read it several times before closing the text. With the book on his lap, he closed his eyes and slowly rocked, picturing the image Jung's description created in his mind. He focused his attention on the sounds his rocker made, the soft creaks speaking to him. The perplexing dream of the previous night replayed in his mind. After several minutes, he opened his eyes, set the cup and Jung's work on the table, and picked up his journal, leafing through it to the entry about the dream.

> Three men wearing breechclouts and moccasins appeared from a fog. The older man had jet-black hair, a hairless chest, and light skin. He stood between the two younger ones. They were darker skinned, thinner, and shorter, but they too sported jet-black hair. With the older man in the lead, the three walked in a dignified manner with heads up and eyes directed toward a large, ochre-colored tepee, which was ornately decorated with paintings of large and small animals, birds, and fish. On either side of the entry flap was an image of a puma raised on hind legs with front paws stretched upward as if leaping for prey.
>
> Inside the tepee, thirteen men, all elders, were dressed in ceremonial attire and sat cross-legged, encircling an enormous fire. Three wood poles, each six feet in height with an iron ring attached to them, made a triangle around the fire. Each of the three men strode to a pole and stood facing the fire with eyes cast straight ahead.
>
> One of the elders, who seemed to be the shaman, rose, and after binding their wrists behind them with leather straps, secured them to the poles. Then he dipped a ladle into a wooden bucket and poured water from it onto rocks inside the fire pit. Immediately,

steam hissed. Next he poured a ladle of water onto the heads of each of the bound men, bowing as he did. Finally, he poured more water on the rocks until the steam permeated the sacred circle.

The elders began to chant in rhythm with a drum, slowly at first, but with increasing velocity and power. Twice more the shaman circled the fire, repeating the ritual of pouring water onto the rocks and onto the foreheads of the three bound men. With that, the twelve other elders stood, and led by the shaman, they began chanting and dancing slowly around the fire and the bound men. They danced around the circle twice more. After the third time, the shaman poured the remainder of the water on the rocks and led the others from the tepee, leaving the men tied and alone in a cloud of steam and smoke.

Daniel lay his journal on his lap and reached again for his tea. He sipped and rocked. Thoughts ran through his mind. For some reason, he had inexplicably associated the three men entering the tepee with himself, Miguel, and Rafael. He pictured Miguel as he thought he might look now and continued to rock. Slowly, his eyes grew heavy. He closed them and focused his attention on the soft whirr of the space heater.

Daniel stood transfixed as he watched Miguel stand before a mirror, fixated on the sheen reflected by the balm spread over Miguel's body. Miguel tensed the

> muscles in his abdomen, took a sharpened blade, and incised a shallow line from his sternum to a point near his naval. Blood seeped from it. In like manner, he made another cut from left to right across it, and blood seeped from that one too. Satisfied with the sign of the cross, he clenched his fists, raised his arms to flex his biceps, and intoned, "Redemption. Cosmic atonement. It is written that defilement of the Father must be redeemed by the Son sacrificing the Father. A lion, courageous and strong, must in turn atone for the Son's defilement. Only blood atones for the defilement. A pyre shall then be lit for the victim. Upon it, he shall give himself up to be immolated, for he understands that he, the Son must, in like manner, purify by sacrificing himself and, thus, be joined to his Father for eternity."

A tap on the door to his room startled Daniel rousting him from his dream.

"Father?" Maggie asked in her light Irish brogue. "Are you still awake?"

"Yes, Maggie," he replied as he struggled to wake himself from his dream state. "I'm just reading."

Maggie opened the door enough to peek in. "I'm so glad you're feeling better, Father. You've had a rough spell of late and you still need to get your rest, so I hate to disturb you. But there's a young man downstairs. He says it's urgent that he see you. He seems very upset and agitated. And not well."

Daniel wondered who it could be, and the thought he had about texting Rafael flashed in his mind. For a moment wondered if it was Rafael but dismissed the thought as too coincidental. It was probably one of his students in distress. But then, maybe not. Maybe it was Rafael. Or Miguel. He nodded to Maggie. "Thanks, Maggie. Tell him I'll be down in a minute."

"Yes, Father. I'll make him a nice cup of tea with honey. That should help calm the lad. He does look sorely upset."

"Thank you, Maggie. He probably could use some mothering. If it is who I think it might be, he lost his mother some time ago and has had a rough life since."

"Oh, Mother of God. I should give him more than tea, don't you think?" Maggie said as she turned and scurried back to the stairs.

Thoughts flooded him as he stepped into the tiny bath to freshen up. He was puzzled by Maggie's brief description of the young man. That didn't seem like Rafael, but then perhaps it was someone else. It was rare, but a few people showed up unexpectedly in distress.

He looked in the mirror and took note of his increasingly gray mane. In the dream, the man's hair was jet-black, but he had sported thick, chestnut brown hair since his childhood. He considered that detail important, but more important was its symbolism. He took a deep breath and left his room. The hall was quiet, and his colleagues' doors were closed. He surmised they were winding down for the day, reading, meditating, or praying. It was Friday and the school year had ended, so they would not need to rise early the next morning to teach, but they generally got up early anyway for vespers in the school chapel. Daniel stepped softly to the spiral stairwell and began his descent.

No one was in the waiting room, but he heard a masculine voice coming from the kitchen. Maggie must have worked her maternal charm and adopted him. Maggie smiled and nodded as he entered the dining room, and Daniel caught the glint in her eye. The young man whose back was to the entryway stood and turned to Daniel.

Daniel shook his head in disbelief. "Rafael?"

"Sí, Padre, it is me."

Daniel barely recognized him. Rafael was gaunt and pale, his skin had an ashen hue, his mouth was drawn and tight, and his eyes bulged. Rafael struggled to stand up. Daniel quickly moved toward him and placed his hand on Rafael's shoulder, gently pushing him back onto the chair. He leaned over Rafael and hugged him as firmly as he dared, and Rafael wrapped his arms around his old teacher and mentor, clutching him as if holding on for dear life. After what seemed like minutes, Daniel stood and stepped back. He narrowed his gaze and scanned his former student while Rafael peered up into his eyes. Those eyes spoke of frailty, like someone facing death.

"You don't look well, Rafael," Father Daniel said as he pulled a chair closer to Rafael and sat. Their knees touched. Father Daniel took Rafael's hands and enclosed them in his.

Rafael shuddered. "I'm not, Padre. It's a bit of a story if you have the time."

"Time I have and always will for you, my son. Let's take your soup and tea into my study. We can talk there."

Daniel turned and saw Maggie had discreetly moved away and was standing just inside the kitchen. "Maggie, please get me a tray to carry Rafael's soup and tea. Also, is there any leftover mac and cheese you baked up for dinner?"

"There is plenty, indeed, Father. I'll warm some and bring it in shortly."

Daniel helped Rafael stand and set the bowl of soup and cup of tea on the platter Maggie handed him. Carrying the tray on his right, he wrapped his left arm around Rafael's shoulders and led him into the study.

"Take that seat, Rafael," Daniel said as he pointed to a tufted Queen Anne.

After Rafael settled into the chair, Daniel set the tray on his lap, pulled the other Queen Anne chair in front of Rafael, and eased back.

When Rafael began to speak, Father Daniel raised his hand, silencing him. "Let's be quiet for a few minutes while you have your soup. It's one of Maggie's secret recipes. No one knows what magical herbs she includes, but I know of its restorative powers from personal experience."

Rafael smiled, lifted a tablespoon of it, and slurped. After several mouthfuls, he said, "It's good. I'm feeling stronger already."

Maggie tapped on the door and came in pushing a serving cart when Daniel bade her enter. The cart carried not only the requested mac and cheese but also a ham and cheese sandwich and a piece of apple pie.

Rafael's eyes widened. "I'm not sure if I could eat all that," he said.

"Well, you eat as much as you can and I'll wrap what you can't. You can take it with you."

Rafael nodded and thanked her. She left the two alone again, and after finishing the soup, Rafael lifted the bowl of mac and cheese from the cart and set it on his tray. He looked up at Father Daniel and said, "She is very sweet. She reminds me of *mi abuela*."

Daniel said nothing but nodded his agreement.

"My God," Rafael suddenly blurted out, "I didn't say grace before I ate."

Daniel smiled widely. "Grace can be spoken through actions as well as through words. By acknowledging and thanking Maggie for her kindness, you offered grace. You see, Rafael, God isn't some distant all-powerful entity somewhere in the distant reaches of space." He pointed to his chest. "God is in here." And pointing toward Rafael's chest, he added, "And in there."

"For me, God is the Great Spirit. It is him I should've thanked."

Rafael took several bites of the mac and cheese and stared at the sandwich Maggie also brought in.

"I don't think I could eat another bite, Padre. It was very good, but my stomach is full."

"I can understand why," Daniel said. "It looks like it has shrunk."

Rafael looked stunned for a moment. Then he lowered his eyes, took a deep breath, and spoke softly. "I'm not well, Padre. In fact, I am very sick." Tears welled up in his eyes. "Padre, I've been diagnosed with HIV. I'm a poz."

Daniel leaned forward and took Rafael's right hand in his. "Rafael, I'm saddened to hear that, but please understand something. You're not a poz. You are a man living with HIV." He paused for a moment then pointedly said, "Got it?"

After a moment, Rafael began nodding, slowly then rapidly up and down as tears flowed down his face. "Thank you, Padre. I needed to hear that. I feel so ashamed."

Daniel leaned back into his chair. "There's no shame in this room. Now, tell me your story."

5

"HIS NAME WAS Enrique," Rafael began. He went on to speak candidly to Daniel about what eventually led to him being infected.

When he met Enrique, it was just sex, but soon he'd fallen in love with him even though Enrique was old enough to be his father. Enrique was kind and generous, bestowing on Rafael beautiful gifts and arranging for Rafael to accompany him to professional conferences. Rafael said it had been exciting, and he'd begun to think highly of himself though he found it curiously strange that Enrique never introduced him to others at those conferences or had him along during the social events and dinners that were part of them. But he didn't mind. It allowed him to explore places he could have never imagined seeing—Seattle, San Francisco, and New Orleans among them.

It was through Enrique, the assistant superintendent and human resources director of a school, that Rafael landed a teaching position, and it was a dream come true. For three years, he taught art at an elementary school. He encouraged his students as his mother and a seventh grade teacher had encouraged him, and they responded with sophisticated works beyond their years. He was loved by the staff, especially the older women who treated him as if he were their own son. No one suspected his relationship with Enrique, which they carefully kept away from prying eyes, especially Enrique's wife.

Rafael had deluded himself into believing that Enrique would divorce his wife, come out to his true self, and marry him. He dreamed of the beautiful home they would build in Cave Creek, furnished lavishly with southwest décor, the walls adorned with his personal works of art. He fantasized about opening a studio to display and sell his paintings to the rich and famous. His art gave evidence both to his dark side, which haunted him, and to the visible side of him through the rich colors of southwest landscapes that bespoke of the desert country's soul. Many of his pieces hung in his teacher friends' homes, gifts from him given with gratitude for their kindness.

Then Enrique abandoned him after his wife discovered their secret. She worshipped in a fundamentalist sect that condemned same-sex interactions and relationships and believed in conversion therapy. Faced with the choice of Rafael or his family, Enrique chose the coward's path and denounced his true sexuality and accused the beautifully youthful Rafael of seducing him.

Rafael's personal world went up in flames, as did his professional world, because he had another secret. He was not licensed to teach, and when that was discovered by the new human resources director, he was immediately fired. Shamed and humiliated, Rafael fled to Palm Springs and began a descent into the caverns of Dante's *Inferno*—scenes from which Rafael had painted to purge his earlier pain—fueled by debauchery. The cruel irony was that he was fated to relive those scenes.

"I got a bit of solace from the experience," Rafael said a bit sardonically. "It's parked outside the rectory. A classic 1972 Challenger. Enrique took care to put it in my name to cover his tracks. It's little consolation, but at least I have something beautiful to be buried in when I die."

"You're not dying," Father Daniel interjected. "And you won't for a long time to come."

The men sat quietly, Daniel reflecting on all he had taken in and Rafael seemingly lost in his thoughts. Even though his eyes were downcast, he seemed less tense than he'd been earlier. Despite the ordeal of revealing his painful truth honestly and without reservation, Daniel could detect a hint of color returning to Rafael's skin. After a few minutes, Rafael looked up.

"Albert Camus, the great French-Algerian philosopher, wrote that when painful truths are acknowledged and talked about, their power perishes," Daniel said. "Earlier you spoke of feeling shame. Do you still feel ashamed?"

Rafael smiled weakly. "No, I don't. Not now. Maybe I was just afraid to tell you."

"Why?"

"I don't know. Maybe because you'd be angry and say you tried to warn me about getting involved with an older man."

Daniel shook his head in confusion. "I did? I don't recall that."

Rafael became a bit more animated. "Well, it wasn't something you said to me specifically. It was during one of our class discussions. We got talking about relationships, and somehow the conversation got into age differences. At first we were talking about men and women, but someone asked about same-sex relationships. And you talked about how older men not only preyed upon younger women but sometimes also on younger men. I felt like you were talking directly to me, although I later realized that was stupid of me."

"No, it wasn't stupid," Daniel replied. "Perhaps it was a warning coming to you from a guardian angel. For whatever reason, it clicked in you and you didn't forget it."

"No, I didn't," Rafael said. "In fact, I kept thinking of that the whole time I was with Enrique. I guess I just wouldn't listen to that nagging voice."

Daniel nodded. "Are you listening to it now?"

Rafael's eyes got wider. "Boy am I ever!"

Daniel edged close to the front of his chair and glanced at his watch. "Rafael, it's getting late, and you have had a long day. I was surprised to see you, even though something told me you were coming."

"Yes, I'm tired, but I'm feeling stronger after enjoying the soup and eating some of the mac and cheese. I drove straight through—fourteen hours. I knew I had to come and talk to you, that you were the only person who could guide me. So I guess I'm kind of exhausted from that."

Daniel gently smiled. "Thank you, Rafael. Thank you for sharing your truth with me so honestly." He stood and gently helped Rafael stand. "Do you have a place to stay? If not, we have a spare room you could use."

"Gracias, Padre, but I'm going to stay with my old friend, Levi. Do you remember him? He was a year ahead of me."

"I believe so. Kind of a brainiac. Loved science. He was really into science fiction."

Rafael chuckled. "Yeah, that's him. We've stayed in touch all these years. I'm going to crash at his place. I guess we'll be up all night catching up."

"Good for you and Levi. He's your friend and that's what good friends are for."

"Yeah. Levi will understand."

"And what about Miguel? Did you contact him to let him know you're back?"

Rafael became rigid. "No. Last week he called and spoke meanly to me. It was the first time we'd talked in a couple of years. He was like a crazy man. I was already feeling bad and wanted to tell him, confide in him. But he just went on with crap, accusing me of stuff I didn't do or know about. I finally hung up on him. I'm not sure if I want to talk to him again anytime soon."

Daniel nodded. This new information took him aback. "Hmm," he finally said as he grabbed the handle of the cart and pushed it to the door. "Come on. I'll ask Maggie to wrap your pie and the rest of your dinner. Then I'll walk you to your car."

When they got to the car, Rafael beamed. "Like it?"

"Well, yes, even in the dark. I can't wait to see it in the daylight. Of course, you'll need to scrub all the bugs off."

"For you, Padre, anything. I'll even put a fresh coat of wax on it."

"That'll be good. And we'll put a fresh coat on you too."

Rafael laughed. "Oh, I'd love a fresh buff."

"You're a devil," Daniel said as he pulled Rafael into an embrace. "Drive safely. Let's touch base after you've caught up on your sleep and feel stronger." He raised his index finger. "You're allowed only one all-nighter with Levi."

"Sí, *Papá.*"

Rafael pulled open the driver's side door. "*Muchas gracias. Buenas noches.*"

Father Daniel put his hands together and bowed his head slightly. "Namaste, Rafael. *Buenas noches, mi hijo.*"

After Rafael left, Daniel waited until he was sure everyone, including Maggie, had turned in for the night before pouring himself a snifter of Baileys and taking it, the bottle, and his phone out to the patio. Even though the moon was waning, it still cast soft light on the scene. It silhouetted the high points of the foothills and softly blanketed the terrain below them. Daniel settled back into the chair, set the bottle of Baileys on the deck, and stretched his legs.

The warm night air was enhanced by the warmth the Baileys provided. It was just what he needed, helping him relax after what he'd learned from Rafael. What Rafael had said was disturbing, but his comment about Miguel was equally revealing. Though Rafael had stayed in off-and-on contact with him over the years, Miguel never disappeared from his memory. It was impossible. Among all his students during his thirty years of teaching, Miguel stood out. He was an enigma possessed by an inscrutableness that defied comprehension.

Apparently, that hadn't changed. Now it looked like Miguel was lashing out, but what made it worse was that it was causing great pain and potential destruction for the two people Miguel likely held closest to his heart. And it was not without danger to himself. He'd unwittingly put himself in legal jeopardy.

That inscrutability was also true of the brothers' differing approaches to life. Though they'd experienced the same cruelties, they responded to them in vastly disparate ways. Antinomy, which he used to describe his own paradoxical being, seemed the apt word for them. They were twin phoenixes that soared up from the ashes of their family history, but they were also polar opposites. Now it seemed these phoenixes were simultaneously plummeting. Could they recover? Once was challenging enough, but overcoming tremendous odds, prejudices, and debilitating life experiences twice? It was a lot to ask of them.

Daniel sipped his Baileys and stared at the yellow-white orb illuminating his immediate world. He reflected on how the moon, an inert composite of space dust, was a vibrant energy source. When it was in or nearing its full phase, the moon could be energizing and inspirational. How many love songs about the power of the moon had been written over the ages? The ancients made a goddess of it, yet it did nothing but reflect the light of the sun. A cumulus cloud floated in front of the moon, partially darkening the landscape, and it triggered a ghostly feeling that was stark and illuminating in its own way. A sudden jolt of awareness moved him. He told himself to get his head out of the clouds. Quit worrying about them and everyone else and focus on your own wellbeing for once, he thought.

Daniel tipped the glass nearly upright and let the last drops of the liqueur slide onto his tongue. He reached for the bottle, poured more into his snifter, and raised his glass to the moon. "To my night goddess."

Feeling snug and safe, he started to drift into a conscious dream state, but a ping from his phone jarred him from his reverie. As he reached for his phone, he wondered who would be texting him so late at night and decided it could be only one person. His suspicion was correct: a text from Mason. Once he'd read it, he closed the screen, put the phone on airplane mode, and settled back again to sip his drink.

A few sips later, he reopened the text, posted a thumbs-up emoji, and hit send. Then he settled back into the chaise and finished his Baileys. Thoughts of snuggling and making love with Mason warmed him further, and he felt an erection coming on. He closed his eyes, placed his hand on his crotch, and whispered, "Whoa, boy. It'll come soon enough." As he entertained the thought of being with Mason, he had to admit that it was the best sex he'd had in ages.

A sudden chill shook him. Daniel opened his eyes and saw it was nearly pitch-black. The moon had been completely shrouded by clouds. He shivered a bit and shook his head, trying to clear it. His phone told him it was close to four in the morning. That meant he'd passed out for about four hours.

He picked up his glass and bottle and made his way back inside. Everything was quiet. Daniel carefully climbed the stairs to prevent them from squeaking and noticed a light under the door to Father James's room as he tiptoed past it. Once he'd eased into his own room and closed the door gently, he stripped to his shorts, pulled the bed cover down, and flopped onto his bed. He closed his eyes and imagined being with Mason as he drifted off to sleep.

6

THE DAY WAS warm and sunny at Red Rocks Amphitheatre, though it hadn't begun that way. It had stormed in the predawn hours, and clouds lingered early on, threatening more rain. But by midmorning they dissipated and blue sky took hold. Daniel met Rafael at the parking lot and together they hiked through the red stone marvel of nature. He was pleased to see how much stronger Rafael appeared after a few days of rest. His skin had a healthier, even robust, glow. As they strolled up to the amphitheater itself, Daniel told Rafael about shows and artists he had seen there, including John Fogarty and Willie Nelson.

"It was the only time I got high," he said, laughing as he described the scene and attendees of Willie's concert. He talked about how everyone was up and dancing as Willie sang and how they all accompanied him by singing along. "There was so much pot being smoked, you couldn't help but inhale it. And of course, Willie seemed to relish the atmosphere.

"That was my favorite concert, but the one with John Fogarty was a close second. The show was fabulous, but what made it especially memorable was when he sang 'Bad Moon Rising.' As he sang, there was literally one of those super full moons off to our right. We all stood and sang along. Everyone kept pointing at the moon when we sang that line about a bad moon rising. It was surreal."

Rafael smiled. "I'm learning another side of you, Padre. I would never have thought of you that way. There's far more to you than I knew."

Daniel grinned mischievously. "I understand. We tend to pigeonhole people and think of them as one-dimensional. I was your teacher, mentor, and adult friend, so you saw me only through that narrow lens. But as you just learned, I'm far more than that. Priests are human and have the same wants and desires as other men. We just cover it up and conceal it behind a black suit and cassock." He poked Rafael in the ribs. "So don't let that disguise fool you."

Rafael raised a curious eyebrow. "So what other aspects of you don't I know about?" He paused before adding, "I guess many."

Daniel pursed his mouth, smiled, and winked. Turning, he pointed to the mountain of red rock that formed the amphitheater. "Let's hike down and around and then we can climb up on some of the rocks if you've a mind to."

"Oh, yeah! This is mind-blowing. I'm so glad you suggested we meet here. I can feel Earth's healing energy reenergizing my spirit. I can't wait to come back for a concert myself, although I don't think it would be a group you'd like."

"You never know. There's only one way to find out."

The two men walked quietly down the road and then headed up the trail to the rocks infused with iron oxide that had been formed millions of years earlier. While Rafael ambled, taking in the grandeur, Daniel was lost in thought. He felt a rising apprehension because he'd planned to share with Rafael the information about his twin brother, but he was now wondering if he could. He wondered how Rafael would react to the news.

At a trail high point, Rafael pointed to a large rock that could be climbed only by an agile rock climber.

"Shall we?"

"You shall if you feel strong enough. I'll wait here."

"I'm feeling much better, and that doesn't look too difficult to climb. I've climbed steeper."

As Rafael deftly scrambled up the rock, Daniel pulled himself atop a boulder and sat watching and beaming. He mused about what it would've been like if he'd had a son like Rafael. He was a complete package of human complications and contradictions: frail, softhearted, caring, imaginative, self-effacing, and vulnerable, yet also strong, determined, and courageous. He then realized an important truth. He had always seen Rafael through that one-dimensional prism too. And just as Rafael was beginning to see him as far more complex than he'd seen him in the past, the reverse was also true. It struck him that Miguel was also more complex than he'd given him credit for being—maybe even more than Rafael.

Daniel gazed upward at the profile of Rafael atop the rock. He was at least thirty feet up and nimbly perched on the precipice. He watched as Rafael stood facing the sun, his arms raised toward it and his head tilted back. Rafael stood there for minutes, neither flinching nor shifting his weight. Not rigid, but solid. Mesmerized, Daniel could feel the spiritual strength flowing through Rafael to him and wondered if Rafael was praying to the Great Spirit, directing his intentions back toward Daniel.

After some time, Rafael lowered his arms, put his hands together in prayer fashion, and bowed. He seemed to defy gravity as he leaned out over the rock's edge. Daniel added *balanced* to the descriptors he had applied to Rafael a few minutes earlier. It was as if Rafael were suspended in time and space, unaffected by the law of gravity. Finally, Rafael turned and nimbly trotted with short steps down the rock. After leaping off the rock, Rafael climbed atop the boulder on which Daniel sat, crossed his legs, and folded his arms across his chest. They sat side by side facing the sun in silence for several minutes.

"I said a prayer for you," Rafael said softly.

Daniel sat quietly before replying. "I felt it. Thank you." He paused and cleared his throat before turning toward Rafael and continuing. "There *is* something I need to share with you, Rafael. It won't be easy for me to say it or for you to hear it, but you need to know. Miguel is in a world of hurt. He was arrested on assault charges."

Rafael jerked his head around to look at Daniel, and the look on his face told Daniel he was shocked and disturbed by the news.

"His boyfriend, Stephen, came to talk with me. That's who he assaulted. Stephen didn't want Miguel to go to jail, but it wasn't the first time Miguel had gotten physical with him. And he knows a good deal about Miguel's past, including the abuse the two of you suffered. So he knows Miguel has issues. He's been concerned that Miguel might commit suicide. Stephen convinced the DA to take his issues into account, and ultimately, the DA gave Miguel the option of having prosecution deferred if he went to counseling."

Rafael shook his head, and his voice was tense as he spoke. "I'm confused. That doesn't seem like Miguel. He was always so confident and strong."

Rafael lapsed into silence, and Daniel was concerned about how what he had revealed might be affecting Rafael. Daniel placed his elbows on his knees, interlocked his fingers, and lowered his head, resting his forehead upon them.

Rafael slid down from the rock and stepped a few feet ahead to stand facing away from Daniel. The air was warm and dry, and there was barely a whisper of a breeze. Under other circumstances, it would feel Edenic. Suddenly, he pivoted on his heals.

"Padre," he said with a tremolo in his voice. Daniel looked up in surprise.

"You said Miguel's boyfriend knows about the abuse we endured. No, Padre, it wasn't abuse." Rafael's face tightened, he shook his head forcefully, and his breathing became so deep and fast that he was almost hyperventilating. "No, Padre, it was hell!"

Rafael looked up to the sky and then back down to Daniel with tears streaming down his cheeks.

"You know only the surface of what happened. You don't know what really happened when our father went mad. He became an animal, a *bestia*! Our father! The one who gave us life. He beat me with a big sex toy and threatened to rape me with it. And Miguel too. He told us if we wanted to be *putos*, he'd show us what it would be like—what would be in store for us. It hurt, badly. Not just physically. In every way. He was our father. We could take his beatings. We understood where they came from. But that ..." He paused, as if considering whether to say something before adding, "Sometimes I wish I'd had the balls to shoot that bastard of a father. I don't know why I didn't."

Daniel sat transfixed listening to the horror Rafael was revealing. Then he slid down from the rock, stepped to Rafael, and pulled him into his embrace. Rafael shook spasmodically. It took all of Daniel's strength to contain him. He said nothing, allowing Rafael to weep, erupt, and spew the toxins from his mind and soul.

When Rafael calmed down and his tremors subsided, Daniel spoke softly. "I'm so sorry, Rafael. I knew it was bad for you and Miguel, but not that bad."

Rafael pulled himself from Daniel's embrace and clutched Daniel's waist as he looked up into the priest's eyes. His face and eyes spoke to Daniel of deep-seated pain and shame.

"Why didn't you tell me? Why keep it a secret?"

"I couldn't," Rafael said as he stepped back. "Miguel made me swear I would never tell anyone. He said it was too shameful to talk about and that we just needed to go on. I wanted to talk about it, but I promised him and swore a blood oath." He became quiet for a time. Then, with a calmer voice, he said, "Padre, I told you about how he spoke to me stupidly the last time we talked. But there's more there too. Worse."

Daniel was bewildered. Thoughts rapidly ran through his mind. That incident and the other beatings must have festered in both boys and both tried to bottle it up and sequester it, with Rafael doing a much better job of containment than Miguel. For all his brilliance and intellectual acumen, Miguel couldn't contain the pain. Rafael had said there was more that was worse than what he'd just revealed, and Daniel wanted to follow up and ask him about it, but it didn't seem the right circumstances given the heightened emotions already at play.

He quickly concluded in his mind that that story could wait until another time. The calm, near serene young man he talked with earlier at the amphitheater and who stood agilely on a high rock precipice had become a torrent of anxiety. His job, he decided, was to lower the temperature and restore a measure of calmness to their discussion.

He took the young man's hand. "Rafael, hopefully this doesn't sound shallow, but I want you to know how sad I feel for you and for Miguel. It explains much. You need help, and so does Miguel."

Rafael's eyes misted. "I know. I finally realize that. I'm so mixed up, and to hear that Miguel might want to kill himself terrifies me. Can you help us, Padre?"

Daniel shook his head. "I don't know. I have to get through a lot of stuff in my own life. I'm not sure I could handle all this well if I tried to focus on too many issues. I can be your friend and Miguel's too, but I don't think it would be a good idea for me to try to be your and Miguel's counselor or therapist. We're too close."

"Then who could help us?" Rafael asked plaintively.

Daniel let go of Rafael's hands and wrapped his arm around Rafael's shoulders. "Let's start down. I know one or two who might."

7

THE RAIN WAS coming down in sheets, and just as he thought it was easing up, it increased in intensity. Daniel decided to sit in his vehicle and wait for the rain to subside a bit before chancing a run across the parking lot. The drive across the southern Denver metro area had been brutal. The storm had let loose during the height of the rush hour just as he was heading up a steep grade of C-470. He felt relieved he was driving to higher ground and not westbound to where there was a good possibility of the highway becoming submerged. Fortunately, hydroplaning was not an issue because the traffic had come to a crawl. After crawling along for a couple of miles, he was relieved to see the Yale Street exit. He would navigate the rest of the way to Mason's apartment via County Line Road.

He'd texted Mason after he parked. "Arrived safely. In the lot. Waiting for it to ease up." Mason shortly replied with a thumbs-up emoji.

Rafael's account of the horrific abuse inflicted on him and Miguel by their father boggled Daniel's mind, but though it was difficult to imagine, he knew the truth of it. He believed Rafael accurately described what had transpired when their father went into a rage. He pictured Rafael standing nimbly and serenely at the edge of that rock with arms outstretched, offering a prayer to the Great Spirit. Daniel offered a prayer for Rafael and Miguel and thanked God for bringing them into his life. "Lord, help me do my best," he whispered.

The torrents of rain cascaded down the vehicle's windshield. The wind had picked up and the gusts rocked the vehicle while loud thunder peals boomed. Daniel felt safe and offered a blessing to all those not so fortunate who were stuck or stranded on the roads. He hoped none were caught in an eddy or standing lake of water at low points. Flash flooding was not a rarity in Denver. When it happened, it was often on a day like this one in which the morning was nothing but blue sky and a gentle breeze but by early afternoon, clouds formed and built up. They were fluffy, white cumulus clouds initially, but they quickly became swollen and heavy. He knew too that the northern part of the metro area might be basking in sunlight while its neighbors to the south were wondering if they might need pontoons to reach safety. Such was the oftentimes crazy, contrasting, and conflicting metro Denver weather.

Just then, like a gushing faucet being turned off, the rain lightened and became a gentle sprinkle. Sunlight appeared from the west through the parting clouds. The storm was heading due east out to the eastern plains and Kansas. Daniel texted Mason that he was heading in. He got out, made a dash to the door, punched in the security code, and rode the elevator to the seventh floor. He knocked and was ready to let himself in when Mason opened the door. Before him was the most handsome man Daniel had ever met. Mason smiled generously and pulled back the door to allow Daniel to enter.

"Thank you for coming over on short notice," Mason said as Daniel stepped in.

"No problem. I had the evening free," Daniel replied. "Besides, I was hoping you'd reach out. It has been a while."

When Mason leaned in and kissed him lightly, Daniel pulled Mason into an embrace and returned the kiss more fully.

"I've had quite an itinerary the past two weeks, including three days in Barcelona," Mason said. "I texted you after we landed back in the States. I'll need to tell you about it. I'm sure you will be envious."

Daniel smiled. "I already am." He scanned the room. "I love how tastefully you decorate. The indirect lighting really softens the room."

"Thank you, Daniel. Thank you for noticing. Please make yourself comfortable. I need to wrap up something on the computer. It will only take a minute." He started down the hall and called back over his shoulder, "Oh, I opened a bottle of Chablis. Pour yourself a glass. And there's a platter with flavored cream cheese and crackers."

Daniel poured himself a glass, filled a small plate with crackers and a scoop of cream cheese, and sat on the black leather sofa. He scanned the room again. It was an image out of an upscale interior design magazine. He gazed at the aquarium with its colorful fish. It too was well laid out and complemented the décor. Everything in the room spoke of perfection and precision.

Daniel knew Mason wasn't perfect despite his attempts to project it. He had his quirks. One Daniel quickly noticed after they met was Mason's obsessive attention to detail. Everything had to be just so. He decided Mason had some level of obsessive-compulsive disorder, but that was hardly a debilitating fault. Compounding it, though, was the fact that Mason was very sensitive to the full range of sensory intakes from odors to color schemes.

But he was also brilliant. He had a bachelor's degree in computer technology, a master's degree in business, and another in childhood psychology. Yet he eschewed all of them as professions. Being a flight attendant was his calling, Mason said, and even though it was a later in life pursuit, he seemed to be thriving in it. For that, Daniel was grateful. It had been challenging to watch his friend bounce from one job to the next over the past couple of months—because another of Mason's peculiarities was that he invariably clashed with coworkers despite being quite affable, gracious, charming, and accommodating.

Mason appeared from the hallway. "I apologize. It took longer than I expected. A ton of emails to go through. And I had to get caught up on Facebook."

"It's okay," Daniel replied. "I just sat and took in the beauty of your place. It's so well appointed."

"I'm so pleased that you helped yourself to the cheese and crackers. I hope you like the cream cheese. It's salmon and herb flavored. I'm not ordinarily a fish lover after having been raised on it from childhood, but that has just the right taste, don't you think?"

"It does. I like it. Oh, and I poured you a glass of wine and filled a plate for you. It's on the end table."

"Thank you. I'm not very hungry, so this might be dinner." Mason sat down on the single chair across from Daniel.

"So tell me about your trip."

"Oh, honey, it was fantastic. It was like nonstop. We flew from Denver to Orlando and then on to Bermuda. Back to Orlando, then up to Montreal. The last part was across to Barcelona. It was simply gorgeous. I had this incredible hotel room to myself. You'd be amazed at all the services they offer."

"Did you go out? Walk the plaza?"

"Oh, we went to this darling little bistro. They had the best cappuccino I've ever tasted. And delicious pastries."

"How long were you there?"

"We flew in on a late afternoon. So we spent that night and had the next day to ourselves to rest up. Then we flew back early the next morning."

"Did you do any touring? I hear Barcelona is one of the most charming cities in the world. So much to do and see."

"My friends went out both nights, but I stayed back. I was pretty exhausted, and the room and all its amenities were to die for."

Daniel nodded. "I see."

A quiet fell over them. Mason broke it when he noticed Daniel had finished his wine and asked if he would like his glass refilled. Once he'd refilled both glasses, Mason settled back in his chair.

Daniel cleared his throat. "So what's on your mind? You had said in your text that you needed to talk."

Mason squirmed a bit in his chair. "Oh, that. It's not a big deal. I was irritated with the lead flight attendant on our flight back. We hit some turbulence, and he didn't follow procedures in accordance with our guidelines. I'm okay now."

"Was everything okay? Anyone get hurt?"

"No, but that isn't the point. Someone could have been, and I told him so. After we returned, I reported him to our supervisor." He paused before going on. "This has happened before. I don't know why they put people in charge who don't know what they're doing."

"Well, Mason, people aren't perfect and even the best make mistakes."

"But that's not okay. When you're in charge, you aren't allowed to make mistakes."

"Did you tell him you were going to report him?"

"Yes. I was direct and honest with him. I told him he was incompetent."

"Hmm. I see."

Mason yawned. "Daniel, I hate to do this, but I need to get some sleep. I'm absolutely drained after that whirlwind itinerary. I hope you don't mind." His phone pinged, indicating he had a text message. Mason glanced at it and flashed a quick smile before sending a quick reply and setting the phone back on the end table. He gave Daniel an apologetic look and stood to indicate it was time for Daniel to go. "I appreciate your making the drive across town in this horrible weather."

They walked to the door and hugged again. "Thank you, Daniel, for coming over. It means a lot." Mason pulled the door open.

Daniel stepped out into the hallway. "When are you scheduled to fly out again?"

"Oh, I have the rest of this week and the first part of next off, but I have lots to do. You understand."

Daniel raised his eyebrows and widened his eyes. "I do."

"Oh, and Daniel, I almost forgot." Mason scrunched up his nose. "Would you be a dear and come by every few days after that to feed the fish and water the plants. I promised my sister I would make it to Shreveport in time for our mother's eighty-fourth birthday. It's right on the heels of my next flight duty."

"Sure," Daniel said in a flat voice. "Anything else?" he asked, trying to avoid sounding sarcastic.

Mason scrunched his nose again, this time as if in thought. "No. I don't get much mail, so I don't think my box will get filled."

Daniel turned to go down the hall and said over his shoulder, "Take care of yourself. Let me know when you're back in town."

"I will. Tata."

Stunned and more than irritated, Daniel sat in his vehicle for a few minutes before starting the engine. Mason's text implied something very serious had happened and he needed to talk. Daniel had been quite concerned, yet Mason seemed pretty calm, even cavalier and evasive. He also seemed distant, as if he was trying to be a gracious host while not so subtly making it clear he didn't want Daniel to stay. It was crazy. Mason was so hard to read. Daniel started the engine, pulled out of the lot, and headed west.

8

I NEED A stiff one, Daniel thought as he pulled into his parking space at the rectory. Scanning the sky, which was now clear in the early evening, he decided it was too pleasant to sit inside. He made his way up to his room, poured himself a snifter of Baileys, grabbed his notebook and drink, and headed down the stairs and toward the back door in the kitchen. Maggie was baking something delicious, and the aroma wafted throughout the downstairs rooms.

"Good evening, Father," she said. "How was your day? We missed you for dinner."

"Oh, Maggie, I'm so sorry. I had an emergency call and completely forgot to let you know I wouldn't be having dinner."

"That's okay, Father. I assumed as much. It's not like you to miss dinner without telling me. Is everything okay?'

"It is. Just someone who needed a good ear. It smells wonderful. Apple pie?"

"Tarts, and they're nearly finished. Are you going to sit out back? Father Richard is out there, and I promised to bring him one."

"A warm apple tart? You're a peach, Maggie, if you'll forgive my mixing metaphors and for not letting you know about dinner."

She beamed. "Oh, Father, I love how you can play with words. You can mix metaphors, adverbs, and anything else when you're talking to me. I'll be out shortly with a platter of them."

"Thank you, Maggie," Daniel replied as he opened the door. He saw Father Miceli sitting on one of the chaise lounges, reading. They exchanged greetings, and Daniel expressed his regrets at missing dinner.

Daniel pointed to the book Richard was reading as he settled into the chair beside him. "What are you reading?"

"*The Prince of Tides*. Ever read it?"

"Twice. It's packed. One of the best novels I've read."

"Well, coming from you, that's quite a testament. Why so?"

"It resonated. Maybe that's the reason I liked it so much. I'm a southern boy by birth. Not South Carolina born, where the novel primarily is set, but close enough. Dixie is Dixie."

Richard looked inquisitively at Daniel. "I don't think I knew that."

"I was born in Florida, but we moved here when I was still a boy. So my memory of my childhood days there is vague."

"Why did your family pick up and move here?"

"Dad was an engineer who worked in and was part of the Apollo program. We saw so little of him. Mother loved the mountains and skiing, so she decided to move the family here. He commuted whenever he could until he finally landed a job with Lockheed in the seventies. But by then, I had enrolled in the seminary."

"Wow! Quite a pedigree. I assume he's now retired?"

"Oh yeah, and back in Florida."

"Interesting. Do you ever go to see him?"

Daniel looked off at the early evening sunlight cascading out over the foothills and took a sip of his Baileys.

When Daniel didn't reply for a few moments, Richard said, "I'm sorry, Daniel. I didn't mean to pry. We've been friends and colleagues for three or four years now, and I know so little about you."

Daniel smiled and looked back at Richard. "No need to apologize, and I'm very happy to share my story with you. Dad and I aren't on the best of terms. He lives in one of those stupidly rich retirement communities called The Villages. That bothers me, and he isn't happy about the fact that I am a priest who is gay. He sees it as completely contradictory and an affront to his Catholic faith."

Richard closed his book and shifted his weight in the chair. "That has to be rough. How about your mother?"

"She's in a memory care facility in Florida. The only person she remembers or recognizes is Dad. My siblings and I are like strangers to her. I pray every day for her to find relief by taking her last breath. So far, the good Lord hasn't answered my prayer."

"Maybe he has," Richard said. "Maybe she needs to spend more time here on Earth, not so much for her but for others. Like you and your dad."

"I hadn't thought of that," Daniel said in reflection. "She's the only reason he and I talk. He might not care for me or my life, but I know he appreciates my calls when I ask about her. I can always hear the melancholy in his voice."

The two priests sat quietly, and a moment later, Maggie came out with the apple tarts on a tray and set it on the patio table.

"For two of my sons," she said.

"Mother," Richard said, "you treat me better than my own mother."

"And that's the way it's supposed to be. A mother's job is never done. Even her adult sons need to be taken to task and occasionally treated with apple tarts." She started back toward the kitchen. "I have chores to wrap up. You two boys enjoy this blessed evening the good Lord provided. Bon appétit!"

Daniel and Richard each took a tart and a napkin and slowly ate, savoring the warm tart sweetness. As he chewed, Richard appeared to be deep in thought.

"Daniel," he said at last, "if it's okay to ask, I'd like to hear more about your thoughts on the South. Your roots are there, and yet you don't seem to have warm feelings for it. I'm curious not only about why you personally feel as you do but also about your thoughts on the culture there. I'm a northern boy, born and raised, and I've never traveled through the South. In fact, to be honest, I've never had any inclination to do so. So my thoughts and opinions are based on third party sources, things like history books, newspaper reports, and movies." He lifted his book. "And now this."

Daniel took a bite of his tart and set the plate on the table. "To me, the South is a land of contradictions. It's a place of great beauty as well as great evil. Its history is intricately woven with human bondage, slavery, and white supremacy. I feel those things have mutated into the culture's genetic code. There's racism everywhere, as we know, but there it's pronounced. Yet most everyone—white, black, and other ethnic groups—seems polite, gracious, charming, and hospitable, which is where we get the notion of Southern hospitality. To me, though, it's a sham, a veneer, a façade, a cover for the darker side of the land. It's a place where some smilingly say bless your heart as they stab you in the back."

He paused and took a sip of his drink. "I realize I might be stereotyping and that my takes and opinions are largely rooted in my family's history, of which I'm not proud. Apparently, among my ancestors were slave owners. It sickens me to think of it in the first place, but it really disturbs me that my family sugarcoats it, for the most part." He chuckled wryly. "Like how so much down there is sugarcoated."

"Like mint juleps and sweetened iced tea?"

Daniel nodded and raised his snifter. "Yeah. You are what you drink. When I was young, my parents always spoke positively and longingly for the South despite living in Colorado. And they both retained their southern lilt. But as I learned more and more about the South's past, the Civil War, and Jim Crow, and as I watched the Civil Rights Movement and the horrible beatings protestors were getting at the hands of the police, I began to see it from a different perspective. When I asked my parents about that, they were invariably dismissive. They'd say stuff like, 'Oh, honey, now don't you go believing all that nonsense they put on TV and in books.'

"They would even defend slavery, calling it a benign and even noble institution in which slaves thrived. I recall my mother once saying, 'We're a peculiar people, and others just cannot understand us. But it's okay. We know the truth, so we just smile and nod and go on about our stuff.' By the time I graduated from high school, I was outraged by it all. I even began to resent their southern lilts. It came across as pretentious, a syrupy singsong to cover the bitter truth they couldn't swallow, just like the iced tea they needed to lace with sugar."

"Daniel, my friend, you're angry," Richard said. "I can hear it in your voice. The intensity. The rising tone. I suspect I've touched a raw nerve, and I apologize if that has hurt you."

"No," Daniel replied. "Yes, it's a raw nerve, but you don't need to apologize. It's high time, as my parents would say, I get it out. So much resentment, Richard. And it goes deeper personally. I can empathize and identify with the millions of African Americans who are descendants of slaves. At least to a small degree. I was never enslaved, but I know what it's like to be shunned, to be treated as a second-class human.

"As you might recall, last year I took a drive through part of the South. I thought it would be a good time given it was the hundred and fiftieth anniversary of the assault on Fort Sumter. I was heading to Charleston from Atlanta to visit a niece and go to Fort Sumter. Rather than taking the interstate, which arced up and over South Carolina, I decided to take the state roads and see the country and maybe meet some people.

"I stopped to get gas at a mini-mart and went in to use the facility and grab a snack. On my way out, just as I was beginning to push the door open, a black man was approaching from the outside. When he saw me, he pulled it open, stepped back, and courteously held the door. He then stepped back behind it. I detected a slight nod from him. I said thank you then held the door to keep it from closing on him. He stood there for a few seconds as if he didn't know what to do. I smiled and gave a quick nod to indicate it was okay. He smiled, said thank you, and stepped inside. I wished him a good afternoon as he went in. At first, I didn't think much of it, but as I drove onward toward Charleston, the power of that scene hit me. The man was showing me complete deference as if I were his superior." Daniel paused and shook his head. "I don't think I will ever forget that or the look on the man's face."

Daniel stared into his empty snifter. Slowly, his face brightened. "Aunt Lucille, my godmother, is my dad's younger sister. She is truly a steel magnolia." He looked over at Richard. "Ever see the movie?"

"Yeah, once. But it's been years."

"The character played by Olympia Dukakis reminds me of Aunt Lucille. She even resembles her. And they have a similar dry wit and tone. I learned growing up that she backed down to no one. She wasn't confrontive, just steely in her opinion and resolve. She and Mother would get into some tangles, but Dad stayed clear of his little sister when it came to political and social issues. She was an activist in the Civil Rights Movement and worked hard to get the Equal Rights Amendment passed."

"Does she still live down there?"

"No, she finally had enough of the heavy, wet climate, she told me, and said it wasn't the actual weather that caused her to move."

"To where?"

"San Francisco. She said her only regret was that she stayed too long in the land of cypress trees and mint juleps and that by the time she got to San Francisco, she was too old to be wearing flowers in her hair."

Richard laughed, as did Daniel.

"I assume she's still alive," Richard said.

"Oh, yes, and as feisty and sharp as ever even in her late eighties. She attributes it to 'clean living.' Not so much churchy moral living, as she called it, but right living. Social justice. People justice."

Daniel looked at his watch, yawned, and began gathering his stuff up. "Thanks, Richard, for listening. It means a lot and helps. But I need to get back to my room. I have a few items to take care of before I turn in, and I want to be out the door right after breakfast."

"Oh, I forgot you're heading to Santa Fe tomorrow. I'm glad you are. You need some time away. Go ahead. I'll take care of cleaning this up."

Richard gathered his stuff and helped Daniel organize the kitchen tray. Daniel gave Richard a hug and said, "Thanks again, my friend. See you at breakfast."

Back in his room, Daniel showered. After toweling off, he wiped the steam from the mirror and stared at his reflection. He hadn't shaved in a couple of days, which was unusual for him, and he focused on the gray that peppered his otherwise brown whiskers. Jonathan liked it when Daniel sported the unshaved look. It gave Daniel a roguish image, he said. Daniel smiled sardonically at the notion and shook his head. He was no rogue. Jonathan, he thought, thou knowest not what demon thou hast freed.

9

THE EXPANSE OF the San Luis Valley opened wide before Daniel as he cruised down the gentle curves of Poncha Pass. It had been a few years since he had driven through this part of Colorado or, now that he thought of it, any part of the state other than the Denver metro area. He mentally chastised himself for being so derelict about accessing this gift that was literally part of his backyard. The few times he had driven through the Colorado mountains, he found it to be renewing and enriching, both mentally and spiritually.

When he first traveled through the high country, he learned to his surprise that it was not all mountainous. Between and among the peaks and ranges were verdant valleys and dells that provided immediate contrast to the soaring peaks. He came to appreciate that vales such as the San Luis Valley were, from his perspective, vastly different from those of other regions of the United States, like the Great Plains where the never-ending expanses became monotonous to drive through after a stretch. But because they were hemmed in with majestic peaks delineating their boundaries, those in the Colorado high country gave one a true sense of liberation, freedom, and detachment.

Daniel sensed a tinge of sadness rising as he reflected on the contrasting Colorado life zones. He thought of how much the Colorado high country was entwined in Jonathan's soul and how he would burst with joy when they drove through it by proclaiming and extolling the magnificence of the mountains. His joy was infectious.

Daniel was culturally and in many other ways a polar opposite to Jonathan. As a city boy, he was comfortable within the urban complex. Traffic noise and population congestion were part of the landscape, and he embraced them as part of a vibrant culture. A favorite song he loved listening to was Neil Diamond's "A Beautiful Noise." Its pulsing, thumping, steady beat was enlivening. Jonathan, on the other hand, could tolerate that scene only for a short while. After a brief stint on the flatlands, he would flee to the quiet embrace and isolation of the mountains.

Daniel chuckled aloud as he sped up on the relatively straight stretch of highway and recalled the scenario he would pose to his students to get them to think of setting and their environmental comfort zones. Jonathan had challenged him with it when they first met.

"Where would you feel more at ease?" he asked them. "Walking alone late at night down a dimly lit alleyway in the rough part of a city or hiking by yourself through bear and wolf country?"

As their discussions raged on, he would lead his students to appreciate the deeper undertones and implications of their answers. It wasn't merely a superficial question, he would explain. It had deeper meaning about their selves, worldviews, comfort zones, and philosophical underpinnings, including religion and spirituality.

That last construct remained a constant friction between him and Jonathan. In spite of his liberal perspective on religious matters, Daniel still clung to his faith from birth. Jonathan had left it in his wake decades ago. Often, Daniel was backward looking with a yearning for times past while Jonathan moved on. Yet they had maintained a deeply personal relationship and bonding over the years. It gave evidence to the axiom about opposites attracting. But how much longer would it be before their opposing natures outweighed and overcame their mutually shared ones?

A sense of self-recrimination overcame Daniel along with a sense of guilt as he made the left onto highway 17 from US 285. For months he had been circumspect with Jonathan. Months? To be honest with himself, Daniel had to admit the feeling of separation had been in the making for years. At first it was a slight crack, but over time the crack expanded into a fissure, which, in his mind, became a fault. Yet it seemed his old friend seemed to be oblivious to the shifting ground beneath him. Daniel entertained the notion that over time, the rarefied air of the mountains had caused Jonathan's head to be permanently in the clouds. That wasn't surprising given their opposing astrological signs: Daniel a Leo and Jonathan an Aquarius.

The sign for the hot springs caught his attention. He was half tempted to take a break from the drive and pull in to see if he could get a place for the night. A soak, as Mason liked to call a dip in a hot tub or spring, would be an elixir. But he had promised Vincente that he would be in Santa Fe that evening. Besides, a soak would only serve as a diversion from the hard stuff he would be delving deep into with Vincente. He sped up.

It was nearing dusk when Daniel drove in to Santa Fe. It was the first time he'd relied on his vehicle's GPS to find a place. Santa Fe dwarfed in comparison to Denver, but he knew Denver intricately. Though considerably smaller, the town—he hated to call it a city—felt welcoming. If he had gotten there earlier, he might have stopped and toured the Loretto Chapel with its famous spiral staircase that legend held was built by St. Joseph. He wasn't sure if Vincente would be up for that during his visit, but he made a mental note to ask him. They had a lot of ground to cover in their conversations, but from experience, he knew such talks could be quite enervating. It was important for the participants to take breaks to, as he put it, get their heads above water.

As he made his way through the town's maze of streets to Vincente's home, he felt a sense of apprehension seeping in. An irony of his leonine personality was that he could be boldly forthright in the face of and dealing with others' challenges. But with his own, he was very cloistered. Perhaps, he thought, it was because it might be seen as a sign of weakness. But a deeper truth was that openly talking about all he had sequestered in his shadow over time, along with recent events that had not been put away there yet, was unnerving. On the surface, he might be Daniel in a lions' den, but underneath, he was a lamb. That he knew, but what was worse was that Vincente knew it. And his old friend and colleague wouldn't allow him to find refuge in avoidance.

Daniel pulled up in front of Vincente's house and looked in awe at the stucco exterior of the minor mansion. Strategically placed cacti, yucca, and other desert vegetation tastefully created a stately scene. Indirect soft lighting gave the front a warm glow. When he left his vehicle and stepped back on the street for a wider view, the dry warmth enveloped him and he heard Vincente call out.

"Hola, my friend. *Bienvenidos* to where God vacations."

Daniel looked up and saw Vincente leaning over the balustrade with a drink in his hand. Daniel beamed and waved, and Vincente set his drink on the rail and started down his driveway to greet him.

"God? Is he here?" Daniel asked as he and Vincente embraced.

They pulled apart and grinned at each other.

"He left this morning," Vincente said. "Said something about taking a train to the coast. I tried telling him the music wasn't dead, but he wouldn't listen."

"Well," Daniel replied, "you know how gods are. Once they get an idea in their heads, nothing will move them from it."

"Amen, brother." Vincente rubbed Daniel's face. "I love your scruffy look. It gives you a whole different countenance."

"Well, that makes one of us."

Vincente stepped back, tilted his head, and looked closely at Daniel as if he were studying an art piece. He nodded approvingly. "Yep, I like it." He motioned with his head toward Daniel's vehicle. "Let's grab your bags and go in. Sophia is dying to meet you." He threw the strap of one of Daniel's bags over his shoulder. "Sure hope you're hungry. We've been preparing the feast of feasts for our honored guest and friend."

"I'm starving."

The soft sounds of the chatter between Vincente and Sophia and the muffled clatter of dinner plates, cookware, glasses, and silverware sifted out to the deck where Daniel reclined on a chaise lounge. They were the only noises that broke the silence of the otherwise still night. A faint glow from the house interior subtly illuminated the deck. With the deck facing the high desert, the light pollution from the town was minimal. The moon was in its new phase, which allowed the stars to pop and sparkle like tiny candles far beyond what Daniel was used to seeing in Denver's metro area. Holding his drink in his left hand, he worked the lever of the chair with his right to slightly tilt the chair further back. Then he took a sip of his margarita and leaned his head back over the top of the chair. It felt good to stretch his neck that way after the long drive.

Soft mariachi music emanating from speakers creatively camouflaged somewhere nearby replaced the chatter and clatter drifting from the house. It enhanced the dreamlike state Daniel had fallen into. The warm, dry night air added to the effect of the margarita, and his full stomach made Daniel feel as if he had gone into another world, one in which he had no time for worry or stress. He took another sip and saw Vincente settling into the chaise lounge next to him.

"I can understand why God would want to vacation here," Daniel said.

"It's a magical place," Vincente replied. "I don't know why I ever left it. What was I thinking?"

"Maybe you weren't."

"Yeah, I was. To the point of overthinking." He took a sip of his margarita and continued. "In high school, I felt I had a calling to enter the priesthood. A family friend who was a Jesuit talked me into joining the order. Occasionally, I think about what I might've done or where I might've gone if I hadn't."

"Regrets?" Daniel asked.

"No regrets. Mere speculation. Besides, in addition to years of heartburn, I did get one life treasure from it all."

"That being?"

"He's sitting next to me."

Daniel smiled, sat up a bit, and lifted his glass in salute. "Back at you," he said as he settled back in his chair and squirmed a bit to get comfortable. "I have to say, I'm no connoisseur when it comes to margaritas, but this is the finest margarita I have ever tasted. Secret recipe?"

Vincente smiled. "It is. A family one that has been handed down for generations. We have a code in our family. The one sin that would get you excommunicated is sharing our secret recipe outside the family."

"I can understand why. I bet you use only the finest ingredients."

"My lips are sealed. Facing one potential excommunication was enough."

Daniel glanced over at him and raised an eyebrow. "You haven't been excommunicated by the Church, have you?"

"No, but I would've endured it if I hadn't been given a get out of jail free card." He sipped and became more serious in tone. "To be truthful, Daniel, I had thought we'd spend this evening just relaxing, but unlike our cloudless sky, you have a heavy one hanging over you. I'm okay with postponing our chat if you prefer, but this seems like the perfect time and setting."

Daniel looked over his shoulder toward the house.

"Sophia has retired for the evening," Vincente said. Then he chuckled and added, "Probably getting ready to climb into bed and read something light like one of Jung's treatises. She's had an exhausting stretch of late. She's just back from presenting a seminar in New Orleans, so she's pretty wiped out. By the way, she was very struck by your presence and can't wait to get to know more of you."

"And I about her. She's beautiful, not only physically but also personally. So warm and embracing."

"Agreed. It's hard to believe she's even more brilliant than beautiful. I'm a damn lucky man, Daniel. But we're here to talk about you, friend. We got the night."

"We do. But I want to talk about you too. I thought I knew you, but from a distance, I've come to realize I know only the surface Vincente. When I look around at this and learn more about where you are in in your life, I'm blown away. As I said, I'm realizing there is far more beneath the surface."

"That's true of you too, Daniel. It's an area you are guarded and most reticent to talk about."

Daniel allowed Vincente's words to lie gently on him. A sense of anxiety arose, but he took a deep breath, gave it a thought for a moment, and let it pass.

"Even though this is supposed to be about you," Vincente said, "I'll open the conversation by telling my story to help break through the barrier, so to speak. I know you would like to know more, and I'd love to tell it. Care to go spelunking?"

"Yeah." Daniel gestured as if he were adjusting something on his forehead. "I got my headlamp on. Lead the way, fearless leader."

Vincente chuckled, drank the last of his margarita, and offered to make another round.

Daniel gazed at the sky and took a deep breath as Vincente disappeared into the kitchen. Almost immediately, Vincente appeared pushing a cart carrying a bottle of tequila, a decanter filled with margarita mix, and a bucket of ice. Daniel looked at him with mild surprise. Vincente noticed his look as he began mixing their drinks.

"The cart is always ready to go. Just need to load some ice into the bucket and I'm armed and ready. Beats walking back and forth."

He handed Daniel his drink and they both took a sip. Vincente coughed. "Wow! I must've put a double shot in my mine. How's yours?"

"Perfecto."

Vincente smiled and cleared his throat. "Daniel, I'm sure you recall the history and circumstances of my separation from the Jesuits. As you know, I was very unhappy with my situation. It wasn't the Jesuits as much as it was the rigidity of the Church. I became increasingly frustrated as I listened to our boys talk about their stuff—from personal to family and social—knowing there was nothing I could say to help them other than tell them that God loved them and things would get better. I was feeling more and more like I was talking to future lapsed Catholics. But there was something more, something else that was poking at me. I couldn't figure it out. All I sensed was that I would never know what it was as long as I stayed where I was. I had to go."

He paused and took a sip of his drink. "I finally discovered what it was, but it took a long time of reading, writing, reflecting, and meditating to make that discovery. I was conflicted. I was in the right profession, but where and how I was practicing it wasn't right. I was kind of like that round peg trying to fit into a square hole."

In rapt attention, Daniel turned to look at Vincente directly.

"That was driven home when I opened my practice here. Almost immediately, I built up a solid client list. That told me I was helping people, but I wondered where I would find the help *I* needed. Slowly, I began to realize that my *clients* were helping me. Their willingness to be open with all their stuff, much of it painful for them to talk about, spoke directly to their willingness to be vulnerable. And that made me wonder if *I* was truly willing to risk being vulnerable. I became aware that I had cloaked myself in impenetrable armor. It protected and shielded me from being wounded or hurt, so I was safe. But it also trapped me inside. Like a knight of old dressed in mail, all I could feel was the armor itself."

Vincente was staring ahead as he talked, so Daniel knew he couldn't see him wince at that last statement. His words were striking close to home.

"At one point, I had an upcoming lull in my schedule, so I decided to look for a conference that would not only be worthwhile, but also give me a chance to escape and engage in some nonprofessional activities. I found one in Salt Lake City that intrigued me. It was a symposium with breakout sessions by noted Jungian psychologists. The topics covered the breadth of analytical psychology, but two in particular caught my eye. One was on Jung's theory of the conjunction of opposites, *coniunctio oppositorum* in Latin. The other session was on the mythological principle of *hieros gamos,* which, as you probably know, is Greek for sacred union. I was always intrigued by the concepts and had read Jung's writings on them, but I never fully grasped their essences."

He turned toward Daniel and scrunched his nose. "I'm not sure if I completely do now."

Turning back to face the open plains beyond his deck, he continued. "But that's okay. Life is, after all, a never-ending process of learning. Or at least it should be. But something profound happened. During a conference cocktail party, I took particular note of one of the presenters. I don't ordinarily approach someone directly and introduce myself. As you know, I'm more an introvert than an extrovert, but something prompted me to approach her. She was, of course, Sophia.

"For some reason, we connected. After telling her how much I enjoyed and learned from her presentations, we exchanged cards. To my surprise, later that evening she called and asked if I would like to have a drink after the conference wrapped up. I can't tell you, Daniel, how elated I was.

"To say the least, I was nervous. I felt like one of our former students asking the most intelligent and beautiful girl to a prom. But it was okay. She immediately put me at ease. As you noticed earlier this evening, she has a comforting charm about her. Our chat went smoothly. We primarily talked about our professional backgrounds, interests, and practices but also a little about our personal stuff. We clicked on multiple levels, but the most amazing part was her telling me her primary residence was in Taos. That was roughly seventy miles from my house, so she lived up the road from me."

Vincente became quiet, and when Daniel glanced over, he saw Vincente staring out into space. After some time, Vincente jolted slightly, turned toward Daniel, and visibly brightened up.

"I guess there's still a lovesick boy buried deep inside," he said with a smile.

That broke the spell long enough for the men to agree to a third round of drinks, and Daniel retreated to the bathroom while Vincente prepared them.

As he washed his hands, Daniel looked at his three-day growth of beard in the mirror. It gave him another look, one that communicated something different than the two-day scruffy look. He thought of Mason. He was always clean-shaven and his hair was never tousled. Daniel thought Mason had the looks and build needed to model for *GQ* and wondered if Mason ever considered it. Then he thought of Jonathan. A sense of sadness and guilt arose within him. He was being unforgivingly distant from the man he loved most. Jonathan and Mason had one thing in common: They both shaved daily. That was it. Apart from that, they were very different.

After Daniel settled back onto his chair and grabbed his drink, Vincente picked up where he'd left off.

"It was uncanny how Sophia bore into my eyes when we talked. But it didn't make me feel uncomfortable. Her look and questions didn't feel invasive or probing. In fact, they were—she was—captivating. For the first time in my life, I felt that someone read me, saw me like no one else. Thinking back on it, I realize it was because I allowed her to. For the first time, the armor came off. But it wasn't like I was baring my soul.

"As I answered her questions, she just sat quietly, listening to what I had to say. When she saw me squirming a bit after I finished and she still didn't react, she smiled and apologized. She said she hadn't meant to make me feel uneasy. She had just heard and learned so much that she was needing a minute to ingest and process it all. I nervously asked her for her take, and without hesitation, she gave it to me. You're incomplete, she said. I asked her what she meant by that and she said it was up to me to figure it out."

"So did you?" Daniel asked.

"Yes," he said after a few moments. "I did." He paused before continuing. "Through my study and research, I've learned that very few people are complete unto themselves. We often call those who are whole unto themselves avatars, gurus, et cetera. I'm not one of them. I'm no guru and I'm no messenger from the realm beyond us. I'm a simple human. I live very comfortably in this world of duality. But I finally realized something: More than a group or institution, I needed another person to balance me and serve as my other half. I was in need of a yin to balance my yang."

"So Sophia is your yin?"

"Yes, but it's more than being a bedmate or compatible partner. She's my wife and I'm her husband, but those are only titles, role-laden classifications. She balances me by giving me what I need but can't get on my own. And it is also true the other way around. She's mystical and gets into a space few can. In return, I help keep her grounded, sometimes by doing something ordinary like surprising her with flowers and chocolate. Or teasing." He paused and smiled widely. "Not to take the story sideways, but I bet you didn't know I was once quite the practical jokester."

"I didn't. You are?"

Vincente laughed. "Was. When I was a youngster, I was an imp. I pulled all kinds of pranks. But along the way, I lost that."

"How? Through maturity?"

"No. Growing up certainly had a moderating impact on me, but the imp part of me never really left. My pranks and jokes became less childish and more devious. It was my religious training that wrung it out of me. Heaven and hell, I learned, are serious business."

Daniel started laughing. A little at first, but as he thought about it more, his laughter became louder. He sat up and swung his legs over the side of the chaise as his laughter became uncontrollable. He put his hand to his mouth to try to muffle the sound, but tears were rolling down his face.

Vincente began chuckling too. "What's so funny?" he asked.

Daniel's laughter began to subside. "The way you said heaven and hell are serious business. It made me think of a very dour priest who was one of my instructors at seminary. There was another seminarian I connected with, and I think the old guy suspected we had a thing going. We did, but he couldn't prove anything. So we would do just enough to raise and feed his suspicions, like being close study mates and putting our heads together or arm wrestling—anything we could think of that put us physically close.

"One day when Luke and I had our heads together at a learning carrel in the library, seriously pouring through some archaic work, he stopped at our table and said, 'You know heaven and hell are serious business.' We were already chuckling about the inanity of our feeble attempts to decipher the text, so when he said that, we both burst into laughter. He was so angry he just stormed away. And that line became Luke's and my mantra. It's what got us through the ordeal. We repeated it to each other when one of us was down."

Daniel picked up his drink and motioned with it to Vincente. "I'm seeing another side of you, my old friend. In fact, I'm learning that you weren't some dour old counselor for angst-ridden teenagers. You are, indeed, a human hologram."

Vincente swung his legs around and sat up, facing Daniel. He lifted his glass in a toast. "As you are, my friend."

Daniel yawned widely. "Suddenly, I feel really sleepy. It's like I'm ready to drop off right here."

Vincente nodded. "It's okay. Catharsis."

Daniel looked at him quizzically. "Catharsis?"

"Your belly laugh. Whatever you had pent up inside of you just erupted. You expunged it."

"Ah. Probably that and the margaritas. I feel like a zombie. I better head to my room. I'm afraid we'll need to postpone my story until tomorrow."

"It's more than okay. Sleep is what you need. Best elixir for a troubled mind. Do you need help to your room?"

"No, it's just down the hall." He smiled weakly. "But I *am* glad I don't have to negotiate stairs."

"*Buenas noches, mi amigo. Duerme bien.*"

10

DANIEL ROLLED OVER and pulled the sheet up over his head trying to block the bright light invading his eyes. It did little good. He squinted under the sheet in the dim light, pulled it back off his head, and gazed at the bright sunlight streaming through the window as he stretched and yawned. When he looked at the time on his phone, he bolted upright: 9:42. The smell of bacon drifting into his room brought him out of bed and heading for the shower.

Once he'd slipped on a pair of cargo shorts and an orange polo shirt and stepped into the hallway, the aroma of breakfast was more pronounced. He could hear soft New Age music wafting alongside the smells and the sound of Sophia and Vincente softly chatting.

There were greetings all around when Daniel stepped into the kitchen, and when he said he couldn't remember sleeping so soundly, Vincente's reply was, "Everything is good about that. We thought you might want to sleep in a bit, so we held off eating breakfast. Brunch seemed to be the ideal way to begin this day."

Vincente placed platters of hashbrowns, scrambled eggs, bacon, and sausage on the kitchen table while Sophia made toast, and they all sat down to eat. "This is spectacular," Daniel said as he reached for a plate. "I cannot thank you enough."

"We're honored to have you stay with us," Sophia said. "I very much enjoyed our conversation at dinner. You have a fascinating story."

"That's one way to describe it, I suppose. It seems to get more complicated each day," Daniel admitted.

"I can understand why people get overwhelmed when complications set in, yet complications and complexities are what make life worth living," Sophia replied. "Even those that are particularly challenging. By navigating through them, we grow and become stronger. But then there are situations that can cause great harm to a person even though they did nothing to bring it on themselves. Those can be most trying."

Daniel nodded as he took a bite of his toast and redirected the conversation. "Sophia. I have always loved that name. It's Greek for wisdom, God's consort in Christianity."

Sophia laughed. "Well, naming me God's consort was not exactly on my father's mind when I was born. Sophia Loren was. I love being considered God's consort, but not as much as I love being Vincente's consort."

"Thank you, my earthly goddess," Vincente said.

"So what prompted you to become a psychotherapist?" Daniel asked.

"As crazy—forgive me for using that term—as it sounds, when I learned more about the symbolism of my name, I became fascinated with the way the human mind works. I took a psychology class during my high school junior year.

My girlfriends and I would have all-night jam sessions during sleepovers, talking about the boys, but not the way the boys thought we were talking about them. We intentionally went out with each other's boyfriend and then compared notes. It was hilarious. None of them ever got past first base with us, but that's not what they told their buddies. All that macho talk. The boys thought we were a bunch of sluts because of the braggadocio they'd spread. But honestly, it didn't bother us. It made us even more curious about them and the way they thought and behaved."

"I can picture that," Daniel said, "even though I never taught girls, having always taught in an all-boys academy. But during class discussions, which were often freewheeling, I would hear stuff like that. All part of the male ego development."

"Yes, unfortunately too many don't seem to move past that stage. So what about you? Why did you become a priest, and specifically, why a Jesuit?"

"From the time I was little, I was enchanted by what was happening in church. I loved High Mass when the choir sang. The rituals. The incense. I can still smell the incense when I think of it.

"When I was in high school, I became more attuned to learning. I loved my English classes and devoured novels my classmates hated. I had a sense that it was all connected. By all, I mean my Catholic faith and the great works of literature. It was as if a thread ran through and connected them. And that thread was people. Like you, I became intrigued about why we do what we do. And stories help us understand and unravel those mysteries. So I decided I wanted the best of both worlds and looked into teaching orders." He paused for a moment before adding, "I finally settled on the Jesuits."

"That seems very logical," Sophia said. "If one looks at faith through the lens of story rather than through a lens that makes it a code of behavior laden with dogma, I can see how the two—faith and literature—intertwined for you." She reached for the coffee and poured herself a second cup. "Forgive me if I'm intruding, but I'm getting a sense you are questioning some of that. It was a tone in your voice and your hesitation when you talked about joining the Jesuits."

"It's okay. You're right about my questioning a lot right now. But it's not about the Jesuits per se. I'm in conflict with the Church. I'm incensed that over the more than half a century since Vatican II, it remains obstinate and refuses to be more open and embracing. And my personal life is very much in conflict with its edicts. But I can't seem to be able to quit, let go, and move on." He looked over at Vincente. "Like my dear friend did."

Daniel bit his upper lip and stared down at the table. A moment later, when he looked up at Sophia and Vincente, his eyes were glistening. "As they say, it's a mess."

Sophia reached over and placed her hand atop Daniel's. "Thank you for trusting me with your truth. I know how much you trust Vincente, so I'm truly honored that you would allow me into your inner life. I won't patronize you by telling you everything is going to be all right and you'll be fine. It and you just might be, but I'm well aware of the journey ahead for you. There is no easy path through. But know I will be there for you if you would allow me to be your companion and accompany you."

Daniel gripped her hand, set his cup down, and reached his other hand for Vincente's. "Thank you. There seems to be no way out, but like many things, the only way out is to find a way through."

"I was thinking," Vincente said, shifting the conversation, "about maybe going to see the famous spiral staircase supposedly built by St. Joseph. Would you be up for that?"

"I would love to," Daniel said. "In fact, I was thinking about that on my way down. How about you, Sophia?"

"I'm afraid I can't. I have a small gathering this afternoon. It's a post-seminar debriefing. But I'd love to hear all about it at dinner tonight."

"Sounds good," Vincente said. "It's settled." He glanced at the clock on the wall. "It's nearly eleven and I have a few emails to tend to. Let's plan to leave at one. Will that work?"

"That will work," Daniel said. "I'll hang out on the deck. I have some reading and journaling I can immerse myself in."

After freshening up, Daniel grabbed his copy of Carl Jung's *Answer to Job* and his journal and headed to the deck, stopping in the kitchen to pour himself a tall glass of iced tea that Vincente had mentioned was in the refrigerator and adding a slice of lemon to it. It was late morning, so the deck was mostly in the sun. But he spotted an umbrella under which he could place his chaise lounge. Daniel set his tea and materials on a table, positioned the umbrella and chair, and made himself comfortable. The tea, enhanced by the lemon, had a prefect tartness to it. He took a second sip and held it on his tongue. It felt rejuvenating. He thought about the nonstop day two days earlier and liked the contrast between it and this luxuriously unhurried one.

When he set his glass down, he opened his journal and looked over his sketches and notations. Viewing them from the distance of time, he could see a man at odds with himself. There was psychological terminology for that condition, but he didn't think what he had drawn and written were indicative of a disturbed mind—at least not deeply disturbed. Perhaps it would be better, he decided, to describe it or himself as conflicted, confused, or struggling to make sense of two parallel truths in opposition to each other. How could he join them? The conjunction of opposites Vincente mentioned: *Coniunctio oppositorum.*

The problem was that there were layers of disunity within and beyond himself in his relationships. Within himself, he was putting his finger on his conflict. But outside, he could identify only half of the problem. As Vincente had been prior to meeting Sophia, perhaps he was incomplete, and as such, he was tearing at himself. That, in turn, served to compound his problem. He would have to make himself whole inwardly to have any chance at completion outwardly.

On his pad, he drew an isosceles triangle. Atop the pinnacle, he drew a straight line. At the left end of the line, he drew an oval and inside it wrote *Daniel.* At the right, he drew another oval. Inside it, he put a question mark. He sipped his iced tea as he focused on his sketch. Until recently, if he'd been asked to fill in the oval, he would've written Jonathan's name. For years, Jonathan had balanced him. But now, in good conscience, he couldn't put Jonathan's name there.

How long could he go on with that oval being blank? Whose name might he eventually put there? Or would it not be the name of a person but a group or something else, like a purpose or mission in life? Maybe service to the underserved? That didn't seem right. It had to be a person. And that thought triggered the most perplexing question: How long could he avoid having the conversation with Jonathan they needed to have? That thought made him feel like crap.

Daniel opened his book to the page he had bookmarked: Jung's explanation of antinomy in the context of the opposition of God to his creation, man. Jung wrote that a Christian had to conclude that all good came from God and all evil came from man. But, Jung argued, that would accuse God of instilling a demonic grandeur in his human creation, which, he said, was absurd to consider.

Strangely, it made Daniel think of Miguel. Daniel wasn't God, and Miguel wasn't a demon. He wasn't evil. He wasn't Mephistopheles. He wasn't even bad. He was, Daniel thought, mad—mad in the emotional sense and to some degree psychologically. That much of Miguel's mental and emotional states he sensed to be true. His past certainly might explain his madness, but something inside Daniel was telling him there was more. Someone or something, he thought, had caused Miguel's mind to become twisted. But who or what?

Daniel shook his head to clear the thoughts and closed the book. He set it on the table, picked up his tea, and leaned back in his chair. I'm getting inside my own head, he thought. He directed his attention to the potted plants and flowers that adorned the deck. They were full of life and rich with beauty. They had good caretakers who helped make them so, yet they were like the lilies of the field Jesus referred to. They neither toiled nor spun. And here am I, he thought, like billions across the world, endlessly toiling and spinning. What was wrong with that picture?

A ping drew his attention to his phone. It was a text from Rafael. "Padre, I need to talk to you, but not on the phone. When can I see you?" A second text quickly followed. "It's good. I think."

Daniel stared off at the field beyond the deck considering what Rafael's urgent need to meet might be about. Just as the thought passed his mind, Vincente came out of the house.

"You have a pensive look on your face," he said.

"I just got a text from Rafael. He wants to see me as soon as possible. He qualified it by saying he thought he might have good news." Daniel looked at Vincente quizzingly. "It has to be about Miguel. I wonder what it could be."

"One way to find out is to call him."

"No, he says not on the phone." He paused in thought for a moment. "Something's up. I need to get back there. Sorry, Vincente, a change in plans."

"No need to be sorry. When do you think you'll head out?"

Daniel looked at the time on his phone. "It's nearly one, so no point leaving now. I'm thinking an early start in the morning could put me back there by midday or early afternoon at the latest. And I promised you that I'd deliver on my end of the conversation. Maybe this evening?"

"This evening would be good. Sophia texted to say she wouldn't be able to join us for dinner after all. Apparently, her meeting will be running late, and the group decided on après-seminar drinks." He yawned. "Let's not check out the spiral staircase this time. I wouldn't mind a nice nap right now. That will keep me from dropping off in the middle of our talk this evening. I'm afraid you wore my ass out last night trying to keep up with you on the margs."

"What? *You* keeping up with *me*?" Daniel said good-naturedly. "I believe it was the other way around. You were killing me."

They both laughed.

"We're like two postadolescents doing shots in a college dorm," Vincente said as he moved toward the house.

"Yeah, the good old seminary days. Please don't remind me."

Vincente turned and faced Daniel as he stepped through the sliding door. "Oh, but I need to. Heaven and hell, after all, are serious business."

They both laughed again. That line would now be a joke he and Vincente shared. He thought about his seminary classmate Luke and wondered where he was. Luke had dropped out of the seminary in his senior year. He had confided in Daniel that he was grappling with too many conflicting notions about faith in general and Catholicism in particular to continue.

Daniel picked up his phone and texted Rafael that he was in Santa Fe at the moment but would be back around midday the next day. He'd text then and set a time to meet. He drank the remainder of his iced tea and lay back in the chaise lounge chair to stare across the open plain. It seemed to go on forever. He could feel the sun beginning to shine on his face. It felt good, not hot but warm and comforting. Things were astir, but for now, there was only calmness. Tomorrow would bring what it would. For now, I'm here, he thought. He closed his eyes and let the warmth of the sun work its magic in bringing him peace of mind.

> The plain beyond the deck seemed different. It had turned more brown, as if parched from a serious lack of rain. He saw Luke walking across the plain toward the house.
>
> "Hey, Daniel, old buddy," Luke called out as he neared. "It's been a while."
>
> When Luke got to the deck, he climbed over the rail, stood in front of Daniel, and ran his hand down the front of Daniel's shirt. "You look good in black. And that Roman collar is so you."

"I'm not so sure about it being me, but it serves its purpose," Daniel replied.

"What purpose? Who you fooling? Everyone sees right through it. The only one you're kidding is you."

"Bullshit. I'm a great teacher and priest. My students love and respect me and so do my fellow priests."

"Bullshit back at you, old friend." Luke grabbed Daniel's shoulders. "Come on. It's me, Luke. We said we'd have no secrets between us. Remember? And that we'd always be brutally honest with each other." He slowly shook his head as he peered into Daniel's eyes. "You're a fraud, friend. Just like I was. I know it and you know it. The difference between us is that you won't admit it."

"I'm not a fraud," Daniel shouted. He grabbed Luke, wrapped his right arm around his neck, and put him in a headlock. Luke stretched his leg behind Daniel, leaned into him, and took him down to the deck floor. The two rolled, grappling as each tried to pin the other.

"What are you boys doing?" their old seminary instructor demanded. You're evil and undeserving to be priests! Get out, the both of you!"

Daniel sat up with a start. He felt groggy, sweaty, and a little shaky as he tried to regain his bearings and stand up. The sun had moved considerably since he'd closed his eyes. He looked at his phone for the time: 3:12. He'd passed out for two hours. What he needed was a cool shower. He turned and unsteadily walked into the house.

Vincente was in the front room, dozing in his recliner, his reading glasses crookedly sitting on his face. A book rested on his lap. Daniel quietly went to his room to shower. The cool water felt rejuvenating. He leaned forward, bracing himself on the front of the shower stall and allowed the cool water to gently flow over his skin. He prayed. *My God, my God, why have I forsaken you?*

11

THE LATE AFTERNOON sun softly lit the horizon beyond Daniel's window. He lay in the bed and stared at the open field. He felt drained and weak, as if he'd just broken a fever. The cool sheets felt comforting. He rolled to his other side and looked at the digital clock on the nightstand. It was just after seven. The house was quiet, the silence broken only by the soft hum of the air conditioning unit.

He closed his eyes, and when he reopened them, the room was dark. A sense of anxiety swept across him. He glanced at the clock and saw that it was 9:40. When he pushed himself up, he could see someone in the easy chair near the bed. A soft light reflected on the face giving it form, but it was not recognizable. The person shifted, reached over, and turned on the pole lamp next to the chair.

"Daniel, my friend," Vincente said. Vincente got up from the chair and sat on the side of Daniel's bed.

Daniel shook his head, trying to clear the cobwebs. "Vincente, I feel like a wrung out dishcloth."

"Just rest. You're exhausted. I suspect everything just caught up to you. Bulldozed right over you."

Daniel could feel a sense of clarity taking hold. "I'm sorry. I didn't come to visit you and crash."

"No need to be sorry," Vincente replied. "Maybe, without realizing it, that's why you came here. You've been on overload, and your body and mind needed to shut down and reset." He gripped Daniel's hand. "You've a long way to go, my friend, and you need to regain your strength. How about a little tea and toast?"

"That would be lovely. Thank you."

A few minutes later, Vincente reappeared with a tray carrying a cup, a porcelain teapot, and toast. He unfolded the tray legs and set the tray in front of Daniel. As Daniel poured the steaming water over the tea bag, Vincente pulled the easy chair next to Daniel's bed and eased back into it.

"I was reading one of my favorite novels," Vincente said. "*Bless Me, Ultima.* Have you read it?"

Daniel shook his head.

"It's a story about a boy, and it's set here in New Mexico out on the llano. The culture is a blend of traditional Catholicism and indigenous folk beliefs. Ultima is the grand-woman of the tribe. She's a *curandera,* a person who specializes in folk medicines, drawing on the power of herbs and other natural remedies to heal. But Ultima taps in to deeper powers that go beyond that of ordinary healers."

He paused and smiled wistfully. "It's strange. When I read that story, I'm transported to that place and time, which wasn't all that long ago. Post World War II. But enough about my reading habits and interests. It's time we talk about you, my friend."

Daniel swallowed the bite he was chewing and washed it down with some tea. "I feel I could use some of Ultima's healing powers right now. You wouldn't happen to know any local *curanderas,* would you?"

"I'm sure I could locate one easily enough. Are you serious?"

"I don't know. I had never heard of a *curandera* until you mentioned Ultima. Sometimes I wonder if I'm possessed. I don't mean by a devil, but something that has gotten inside me and taken control. I know that's not the case. I can't duck responsibility and foist the blame for my behavior onto some entity that has taken control of my psyche. But in a strange way, it helps to personify it."

"When it got later into the evening and you hadn't come down to eat, I came by. I thought I heard you talking to someone. At first I thought you had a call, but for some reason, that didn't feel right. I tapped on the door and called your name, but you went right on talking. I opened the door a crack and what I heard was like gibberish. You were speaking in English, but it was very incoherent and nonsensical. I could see you tossing a bit, like you were wrestling with someone. I thought to awaken you, but then thought better of it. Whatever you were processing from your unconscious through your dream had to be worked out. After a while, you suddenly stopped, relaxed, and seemed to fall into a deep sleep. Your breathing became slower and softer.

"I went and got my book and little reading light. When I got back, I could see you hadn't moved, and you didn't for the next couple of hours. I could hear you breathing softly, but that was it. You didn't stir, snore, or anything until you suddenly woke up."

Daniel narrowed his eyes and stared at the sheet he was fingering. "I don't remember what I was dreaming just now, but this afternoon, when I was out on the deck, I dozed off and had a dream. It was very disconcerting. In it was the seminary friend I told you I had gotten quite close to, intimate, in fact. His name was Luke. He came walking across the plain toward your house. The next thing I knew, he was on the deck in front of me. At first he was friendly. He got close and stroked my shirt and told me I looked good in black with my Roman priest collar. But then he told me I was a fraud. I grabbed him in a headlock and we started wrestling. We fell to the deck, where we grappled with one another. Then that uptight old priest came and yelled at us." Daniel looked up at Vincente. "That was it."

Vincente sat quietly as Daniel talked, and he seemed enraptured with Daniel's story.

Daniel poured himself another cup of tea, took a sip, and leaned back. Again he focused his eyes, this time staring at his feet protruding from under the sheet. Taking a deep breath, he turned toward Vincente and bored directly into his eyes.

"I met this guy a few months ago at one of those saunas at a rec center. His name is Mason. He was sitting on the steps above the pool wrapped in his white towel. As soon as I saw him, I was struck by how handsome he was. There was something about him, like some energy, an aura emanating from him. He projected a dignity about himself, even in the way he sat. He wasn't slouching but instead sat erect, but not rigidly so. Everything spoke of perfection. He looked like he had just gotten one of those hundred-dollar haircuts. It was perfectly coiffed. His nails were manicured and his skin was slightly tanned. It contrasted well with his white towel. His physique wasn't solid muscularly, but he was fit. Tall and not too thin. I tried to be discreet, but it became obvious I was staring at him. Finally, he stood, came over, and sat next to me. He said hello, and I've been a mess ever since."

Daniel became quiet, searching in his mind about where to go next. He knew there wasn't anything he couldn't trust Vincente with. But it wasn't a matter of trust. Nor was it a matter of courage. Daniel surmised that he felt shame: He was ashamed of admitting to weakness, to caving in to temptation and engaging in salacious behaviors. He had made a farce of his vows, especially the one about remaining chaste. He'd never felt that before. The intimacy between him and Jonathan had seemed pure. At least that was how he justified it. But this, what he was about to own up to, was beyond the bounds of propriety. Or so he thought. Daniel knew his friend was not going to allow him to skate and escape. Vincente would hold him accountable.

Vincente waited for him to continue, but after a few moments, he broke the silence.

"It sounds like Mason is handsome and charming. His beauty, though, is only skin deep and his charm could be a front. So what about him? I'm sure you've gotten to know him quite well over the past few months."

"I have, and I've gotten to know myself better too. That's where it gets complicated."

There was a pause in the conversation, and Daniel began to notice how dark the room seemed and how stale the air felt. He needed to get out of bed and had an urge to go outside for the telling of his story about Mason. When he proposed they move the discussion outside, Vincente was in agreement and went off to make a snack tray while Daniel washed up a bit.

After settling into their deck chairs, Daniel filled his plate with cheese slices, chips, and other munchies from the meat and veggie tray Vincente had thrown together. The iced tea with lemon slices, which Vincente had thoughtfully made decaf, felt refreshing.

"Where to begin?" Daniel said. "Like I said earlier, it's complicated. I told you a bit about Mason, but he wasn't the first man I got together with, though he did something no other man has ever done, other than Jonathan. He captivated me. You commented about his beauty being skin deep. That's true, but it's also not true. He has an inner beauty, but it is so scarred and mutilated that you have to dig to find it. You need to peel away the layers he's built around it.

"Mason is very handsome physically. His face is well sculpted and well proportioned, he has the bluest of eyes, and his hair shows only a hint of graying. And those things are enhanced by his sense of style. He has a keen eye for color and a sophisticated sense of fashion. Yeah, it is a veneer, and it does a phenomenal job of hiding or disguising his true self. It helps to conceal his inner turmoil.

"Mason has deep issues. He's bipolar and deals with bouts of depression that can overwhelm him and keep him from functioning. And I suspect he's dealing with Asperger syndrome. He's ultrasensitive to touch and sees colors I can't detect—like shades of blue that have a tinge of red or green or some other color. I swear he could look at a paint chip or cloth swatch and tell you which colors were mixed to make that tone and how much of each is in it. He's kind of like the guy in *Rain Man* who could instantly count the number of matchsticks that fell to the floor. Like a form of autism."

"Is he on meds? Does he see a therapist or psychologist?"

"He is and he does, but that's all I know." Daniel picked up his glass of iced tea and took a long draught from it. "Yet he's the most wonderful human being when he's got himself together mentally. Or at least used to be. When we first met, we'd go out for dinner or catch a movie. He loves movies, by the way. He could sit for hours and watch all kinds of films, but mostly he likes musicals and uplifting stories. He has a deep romantic side to his character."

"What about his past? His family?"

Daniel shook his head. "Not good. He grew up in an upper middle-class culture. He never wanted for anything. But his family is very fundamentalist. Mason told me that from the time he was a little boy, he thought he was gay. He didn't know the word then, but he knew he liked boys. He believes his father suspected that, so he treated Mason roughly, even humiliating him in front of others. So Mason did everything he could to hide it. He dated girls throughout high school, and after graduation he went to divinity school for a couple of years. Later, he married one of the girls from his high school class who was a beauty queen of sorts. It was a high society affair and drew all kinds of attention and approval from the upper crust. But inside, he was miserable, which in turn led to a nervous breakdown."

Daniel paused to drink more of his iced tea while trying to calm himself. He could feel himself becoming angry on Mason's behalf, but he knew his ire wasn't just about Mason's situation.

"It's not right," he finally sputtered. "I get angry enough when I witness or think about the hypocrites that pervade religions, but I go ballistic when I witness the harm they cause. Mason was brutalized psychologically as a growing boy, which led him to make serious mistakes as he moved into adulthood that caused him great pain. He shielded himself, trying to hide his true nature. But in time, it had to come out, and it did."

Vincente didn't reply immediately, and the resulting pause in the conversation allowed Daniel a little time to let his anger subside.

Vincente finally spoke. "What kind of man has Mason become?"

Daniel lifted his head to look at Vincente through glistening eyes. "A not very nice one of late. At least underneath. On the surface, when he's not overcome with depressive emotions, he can turn on the charisma and still be his charming self. But I see right through it." He took a deep breath. "I see him now for what he has become: a user. And that's the most difficult part of it for me right now. I know that, but I can't seem to stop being used. I can't even stop *wanting* to be used."

"Was he a user when you met him?"

"I don't know. He might've been. He once told me he'd taken acting lessons and actually played a few roles in local theaters when he was in high school and college. So maybe it's an act he's perfected and I was blinded by what I saw on the surface."

"Do you ever think about just refusing to take his calls and texts and not seeing him?"

Daniel grimaced. "I have, but I can't. I don't know why, but I can't. I think of that line in *Brokeback Mountain* about why the one guy couldn't quit the other. Same with me. I can't seem to quit Mason."

Daniel shrugged. "I guess the follow-up question is why not. I think it might be for one of two reasons or both. In some way, a way I can't put my finger on exactly, I identify with Mason. We're from the same area of the country: the South. We have similar educational experiences. We're different too, but in ways that complement each other. His interests and talents lie with art, and mine lie with literature. Different mediums but both forms of personal expression. And of course, we're both gay, and like most if not all gay men of our generation, we've had to deal with rejection, shaming, and abuse. But there is something deeper with him, something I never felt with another, including Jonathan. I wish I could tell you what it is, but I can't." He shrugged again. "But maybe in time you could tell me."

"Maybe. But I know of another who would be better at helping you break through the barriers."

"Sophia?"

Vincente nodded. "Daniel, you are more than a close friend. You're my brother. In fact, I feel closer to you than I do my own brothers. Which means I will always have blinders on. And my feelings toward the Church are, let me say, more antagonistic than yours. I'm not telling you to share your story with Sophia, nor am I encouraging you to. I'm simply encouraging you to consider it. I have no doubt she would be willing to take you on as a client. But you said there were two reasons you couldn't leave or, as you said, *quit* Mason."

Daniel bit his lower lip. "There are, but the second reason is about me, which is the person we're supposed to be talking about. There's something in my makeup that makes me stay and hang in there with certain people even when the going gets rough. I don't know why, but I simply cannot abandon someone I care for who has been deeply wounded. Maybe it's the abused puppy syndrome."

"Daniel, you're not telling me something I don't already know. I watched you for years taking on and hanging with students everyone else had thrown their hands up on in exasperation. I've seen you work wonders, minor miracles. But you need to understand that you can't save everyone."

"But I can try, can't I?" Daniel replied cautiously.

Vincente gave him a stern look. "Yes, you can, but there will come a time when it will be to your detriment and maybe your undoing." He leaned forward in his chair and firmly gripped Daniel's wrist. "Sometimes you just have to let go."

When Vincente released his wrist, Daniel looked down at his hands and the glass of iced tea he was holding. He began turning the glass in his hands and shook it a little. The power of Vincente's words overpowered him. Vincente had never confronted him or spoken to him with such vigor and intensity. In fact, Daniel could not recall anyone ever talking to him so directly and forcefully in a caring manner other than Jonathan.

"I guess this is what we have come to call an intervention," he said.

Vincente said nothing but kept an unwavering gaze toward Daniel.

After a few moments, Daniel spoke. "Vincente, a few minutes ago, you described my feelings toward the Church as less antagonistic than yours. My feelings are antagonistic, but they're a different level of antagonism from yours, I believe. I suspect that by leaving the Church, you were more than expressing your frustration. You were saying, in essence, that the Church could not be saved. That it wasn't worth the time and effort to work within it to change it for the better. Maybe I'm not being fair about your reasons, but that's what

I concluded from our talks when you were going through your ordeal. I'm not sure I'm there, at least not yet. I struggle with that conflict daily."

"Then why are you seriously considering resigning from the priesthood and renouncing your vows?"

Daniel took a deep breath. "Because I've already renounced my vows. Not formally but in practice. I took a vow of poverty, chastity, and obedience. The last one is the only one I have honored within reason. My aunt, who I was very close to, recently established a trust fund for me contingent on my leaving the Jesuits. Let's just say it's worth far more than six figures. And chastity? I've made a joke of that vow almost from the day I took my vows. It's a sin I commit almost seven days a week, sometimes multiple times a day in thought."

"Proverbs says the just man falls seven times but rises up again," Vincente replied.

"True, but it also says the wicked shall fall into mischief. And if what I've fallen into isn't mischief, I don't know what is."

"I do, and what you've done is not evil. It's human, and you've hurt no one."

"Vincente, I like to think that what I do is not who I am, but it's hard not to think the two are inseparable. I am what I do."

"I disagree. We must separate ourselves from our actions. That's the core of personal conflict. You're struggling with yourself. It's the cause of your anxiety. If you were not only comfortable and content with your behaviors but also proud and open about them, you wouldn't be struggling. You'd be whole. But for some reason, you're doing stuff that conflicts with your being—your psyche, soul, and spirit.

"Daniel, I will be the last one to advise you about what decision to make. Some, like your archbishop, might feel a sense of schadenfreude and rub their hands with glee if they learned about how you are struggling. But the rest of that Proverbs passage warns about that too."

Daniel sighed and looked over at Vincente. "This might seem like I'm changing the subject, but I'm not. Do you believe in the power of dreams, that they are messages from the unconscious that are full of meaning?"

"I subscribe to Jung's theory that they are that and more. Unlike Freud, Jung insisted that dreams can be predictive. So maybe they're not only giving you insight into yourself, but also providing directions as you forge your way through this experience."

Daniel considered what Vincente was saying and nodded. "As you know, I experience powerful, vivid dreams. I write about them in my journal. The interesting thing for me is that my dreams are generally not chaotic ramblings with disparate characters in unlikely situations or places. They tend to be like short movies with real characters in my life. Lately, I've had a few like that, one in which Miguel played a prominent role and another in which a character was likely him. I'll tell you about them later, but I had another one a couple of weeks ago that I haven't been able to sort out, and for some reason, I feel it has meaning for me in my present dilemma.

"In it, I was like Daniel of the Old Testament, locked into a spacious underground cavern with six male lions. They were beautiful, majestic beasts. Dignified in appearance and powerfully built with full fluffy manes. Their hides were a golden color instead of the yellowish-brown they usually are. The cavern was strangely lit with soft yellow lighting, and the air was quite warm and carried a heavy musky odor. There were huge boulders around the perimeter, and two lions lazed atop a couple of them. The others lay on the cavern floor. They occasionally yawned, licked themselves, and swished their tails. But other than that, they lay languorously.

"I found myself not being afraid even though they, like every feline, can have an unpredictable, vicious side if triggered. In fact, I wanted to get closer to them, to touch and even pet them. I got up from the rock I was sitting on and approached one. He didn't move, growl, or make any aggressive move. I got in front of him, stretched my hand out, and tousled his mane. As I did, he purred in a deep sonorous tone and squinted his eyes, just like a little kitty lying atop a person's lap does when it's petted. When I pulled my hand away, he flicked his tongue and licked it. I went around to the other five and they did the same thing. I even lay down next to one. I not only was unafraid, I also felt I belonged there with them. After a bit, I climbed back up on my rock, pulled my knees up to my chest, and wrapped my arms around them. I didn't want to leave. It was as if I belonged there."

Daniel looked over at Vincente. "You're the psychologist. You've studied dreams. Tell me, what does it mean?"

Vincente shook his head. “Well, my friend, I’ll give you the same response Carl Jung gave his patients: I don’t know. But I know someone who might be able to help you unpack them all. And we’ve talked about her.”

Daniel nodded. “You’re right. It’s time Sophia and I talked.”

12

HE HAD PROMISED Rafael that he would be back by midday, so Daniel decided to take the quickest route back to Denver. Google Maps said the drive was about five and a half hours. He figured that with only one pit stop, he could do it in five.

Before pulling out of Vincente and Sophia's driveway, he'd texted James and Richard to give them a heads-up that he'd be returning sooner than expected and would be able to take part in their weekly post-lunch commune session after all. He also asked them to tell Maggie so she'd know he'd be there for lunch. He pulled onto I-25 and headed north and glanced at the time: 6:13. About three hours to Raton Pass, he calculated. Traffic was minimal and most of it was heading south. He glanced at the speedometer and saw he was cruising at seventy-five miles an hour and increased his speed to seventy-eight.

His mind jumped back and forth between reflecting on his conversations with Vincente and guessing at the news Rafael would give him. Rafael had said it was positive—at least he thought it was. That eased Daniel's mind. He also thought about his dream of Luke when he dozed on the deck and how it shook and discombobulated him. The other dreams he'd had needed interpretation, but that one was an in your face truth. No need to interpret Luke's words. He was a fraud.

He was either blessed or cursed with the inordinate ability to vividly recall his dreams long after he woke up. He had told that much about himself to Sophia as they briefly chatted over the early morning breakfast Vincente had put together. She said she would be honored to work with him. It was most fortunate that she was licensed to practice in Colorado and shared an office with another therapist in the Denver suburb of Littleton. A dream come true, he thought, and laughed at himself over the triteness of his summation. But then, maybe it wasn't a dream come true as much as it was one of those synchronistic events Jonathan often talked about. He was a bit amused at the thought that Jonathan had gotten into his head.

Jonathan. As he sped northward, Daniel berated himself for the callous indifference he had been showing him. He wondered why the maxim that we tend to hurt the ones we love most seemed to be more spot on than any other. No one loved Daniel more than Jonathan, and Daniel loved no one as much as he did Jonathan. But were their loves for each other of equal weight and power? Was he, Daniel, incapable of the deep love from the heart and soul that Jonathan obviously felt and showed for him? That never tiring, always forgiving honest type of love? The Greeks called that type of love *agape.* Not only did Jonathan hold that kind of love for Daniel, he held it for everyone else and everything else, from his students to animals, nature, and Earth itself. Was he putting Jonathan on a pedestal, endowing him with Christ-like attributes? If so, was he getting ready to crucify him? Daniel shook his head to clear it, realizing he was overthinking and overanalyzing it.

Taking a deep breath, Daniel glanced at the speedometer and saw he was going eighty-eight miles per hour. He eased off the gas and grabbed the mug of tea Vincente had made for him for a sip. Then he looked up to see two state trooper vehicles sitting in the median. He gently tapped the brake, saw that he was doing only seventy-two, and breathed a sigh of relief after passing and not seeing one of them pull out in pursuit. Shooting a glance toward the car roof, he whispered, "Thank you … whoever."

Daniel again increased his speed to seventy-eight. It was easy to do even though the elevation was rising as he approached Raton Pass. In a few minutes, he'd be in Colorado. For some reason, that idea felt comforting. He thought again of Jonathan and the love they'd had for each other over the decades. Elevating Jonathan to a Christ figure was over the top, but nonetheless, Jonathan did model that type of love more than anyone he knew. In return, all Daniel could muster was the baser forms of love: *philia,* affectionate love, and certainly eros or erotic love.

Daniel searched his mind. There was another Greek word for the type of love that represented their long-term relationship and commitment to each other. He drummed his fingers on the steering wheel and grabbed his tea again. After several sips, it came to mind. *Pragma.* Forever and a day love. They shared that, to be sure, but would it be enough to withstand the tempest and torrents that would soon envelope them?

After crossing the state line into Colorado, Daniel felt the tension he was holding ease to the point that he felt almost relaxed. With his right hand, he fumbled through the CDs strewn across the passenger seat. Quickly glancing down toward the pile, he finally saw the one he was searching for: T*he Paul Simon Songbook.* He popped it from its case and slid it into the CD slot. When the first song, "I Am a Rock" played, he sang along, and when it finished, he clicked the CD forward to the other Paul Simon song that resonated so strongly for him, "Flowers Never Bend with the Rainfall." He sang along with that too. When it finished, he turned the volume down, forwarded the CD to the beginning, and allowed it to play through as he drove toward home with Paul Simon lyrics and soothing vocals sinking into his spirit.

With the school year having ended, the three priests took their time partaking of their Friday midday meal of grilled cheese sandwiches and tomato soup. Daniel gave them a synopsis of his trip and visit with Vincente and Sophia without giving them the specifics of his private conversations with Vincente. Although he implicitly trusted both James and Richard, Daniel was wary about divulging too much of his plight for fear they would jump to conclusions—ones that seemed imminent and preordained but still had not been reached by him. He sensed there might be something afoot given the slightly odd manner in which his friends were reacting to him. James and Richard seemed to be gingerly probing about what had been happening.

"Shall we retire to the study?" James asked after they finished eating.

James, Richard, and Daniel carried their coffee and tea to the study and made themselves comfortable in their preferred chairs. The weekly parley was a tradition James had started a few years earlier. It gave the brotherhood a chance to converse about matters from private and personal to professional and philosophical. During the academic year, they generally met after lunch on Saturdays, but when classes were not in session, Friday seemed the optimal day.

After they got seated and had breezily chatted about the simple but delicious meal they'd just eaten, James cleared his throat and spoke. "Daniel, ordinarily I would not be so direct in what I'm about to say. Most people quaver at blunt talk, but I know you, Daniel, and I believe you would see through my words and resent it if I'm not being direct." He paused before continuing. "We understand the need for you to be careful about sharing details during lunch and with Maggie being in earshot, but it's time for you to be forthright with us."

Daniel nodded. "Brothers, you're right about it being necessary to update you. As you sense, much is going on with me. It is, to be honest, a bit of a crisis of faith for lack of a better way to frame it. But it's not just that. I'm questioning much in my personal life." He smiled sadly. "I guess it's hard to imagine a priest with a personal life, but I think you can relate in your own way. The strain has been quite debilitating, mentally and spiritually. You're aware of the visit I had from Rafael, my former student. We're going to talk this afternoon. It's the main reason I cut my trip short. He texted me yesterday. He was anxious to talk to me in person and said it was good news, or so he thought."

Richard leaned forward in his chair. "Thank you, Daniel. Any news you can share will go far in alleviating our concerns. We respect your privacy, but please remember that we are a brotherhood. We keep our conversations in the strictest confidence. And I want to be careful here because I don't mean to imply anything. But I also want to remind you of the sacred confidentiality of the confessional. Now, I'm not saying you should avail yourself of it with me or James. This is just a gentle reminder of it."

Daniel lowered his eyes and stared at the cup of tea he was holding. He had much to confess, to own up to, if he could only put his finger on what exactly his sins were. He looked over at Richard and nodded.

"Daniel," James said, "Richard and I have talked this through at considerable length. As Richard said, the three of us have been in our own little brotherhood for several years. We've come to know each other intimately: what makes us tick, what pushes our buttons, what our strong points are. In our opinion, there is no doubt that you have the most formidable, dauntless spirit and mind. But we have come to believe that you are like everyone else. You have a blind spot, and it's the deadliest of sins."

He paused, cleared his throat, and continued. "Daniel, we believe you have a pride about you that makes you think you're invincible. As I have pondered and prayed on that, I thought of the irony that a pride is a group of lions, and if you share anything with our animal friends, it's courage. I wonder if there isn't some sort of correlation between lions' pride and a lion's pride.

"Daniel, Richard and I have observed you for years. We have marveled at your gift of perception. You seem able to see into someone's mind and feel their thoughts. But while that has been helpful for so many souls, it has, we are afraid, given you a sense of invincibility—one that makes you think you can never be harmed."

Richard took up the point. "I completely agree with James, Daniel. As he said, we have talked about this extensively. Over the years, I've come to see you as a mentor, personally and professionally. When the boys come into my guidance office, they invariably share with me how much they admire—even worship—you. And while connecting with teenage boys filled with angst and conflict is an amazing energy to have, it can also put you in dangerous situations because in the end, as James noted, you are still human, mortal, and dependent on God like the rest of us."

Daniel squirmed in his chair and shifted his weight. "Brothers, I cannot contest anything you've said. You've spoken honestly and directly, and I appreciate that. You're also right about there being far more to my plight than I have let on. Things are falling apart, and I have no idea how they can be put back together." He exhaled audibly. "I'm seriously considering asking the Holy Father to grant me a dispensation from my vows."

James and Richard stared at him in stunned silence. Daniel eased back into his chair, picked up his cup of tea, and sipped, allowing the men a chance to process what he'd just revealed.

After a few moments, James spoke. "Daniel, so many thoughts are racing through my mind and so many feelings are coursing through my heart. I have questions, but now is not the time to pepper you with them. In due course, you will answer them and my feelings will do what feelings usually do—evolve. That aside, how can I … how can we … help?"

"Brothers, right now you are helping in a way that is most critical. You're giving me a safe haven physically, mentally, emotionally, and spiritually. You're my friends and companions, and without you, I'm not sure I could navigate the waters ahead."

Richard sat up and leaned forward in his chair, setting his hand on Daniel's knee. "Well, my friend, James has expressed how I feel too. So know one thing as you course along. As they say, we have your back."

The three stood. Richard pulled Daniel into a bear hug, and after he let go, James embraced him warmly. Daniel could feel his old friend James stifling sobs.

"So you're off to visit with Rafael?" James asked through misted eyes as he stepped back from the embrace.

"I am. Then tomorrow I plan to see another to whom I must confess far more than I have with you … and ask for his forgiveness."

13

DANIEL SPOTTED RAFAEL perched on the same rock they'd sat on before. He climbed up beside him, pulled his legs up, and wrapped his arms around them. After greeting each other with smiles and nods, neither spoke, and the quiet and stillness was profound. The sky to the east was clear, but large cumulus clouds overhead presaged late afternoon storms. An occasional welcoming breeze stirred the calm and softened the heat.

"I'm so sorry, Padre," Rafael said. "I cannot say that to you enough along with thank you for being here for me. I guess if there is one good thing that has come out of this, it is that for the first time, Miguel and I had a real good talk about what we went through. It wasn't easy getting there. He harbors so much pain, and it blinds his judgment. I'm still in pain too. It's hard, and I keep struggling with it. But I'm not like him. I don't want to hurt other people." He paused and then added, "Only myself."

The priest let go of his grip around his legs, reached over, wrapped an arm around Rafael's shoulder, and pulled the young man toward him. Rafael leaned into him and rested his head on Daniel's shoulder, but after a few moments, Daniel released his embrace and Rafael sat up.

"I guess I tried to bury my pain and the horror of my childhood, but like a zombie, they refused to stay underground. I can see now how stupid it was of me."

"No, not stupid," Father Daniel said. "Very human. When our psyches are overwhelmed with trauma, they can become incapacitated. So to go on and function, we relegate that trauma to what is called our shadow. The problem is that our shadow can become heavy over time. Imagine it like a sack of stuff you're dragging behind you everywhere you go. The more you load stuff into it, the heavier it becomes. It weighs you down, and at some point when the trail becomes very challenging, you come to a halt.

"That's what happened to you, and instead of trying to unpack and lighten that load, you chose to numb it with sex and alcohol. So in a way, you self-combusted. Miguel, though, exploded outward. That's just my assessment. I'm not a trained psychologist, so the best I can do is make an educated appraisal of how the three of us got to this point."

"Padre, I never told anyone this, but I'm telling you now. Miguel tried to kill me once. It happened a few years ago. It was why I left Colorado and fled to Arizona. To get away from him. We were at a Cinco de Mayo party where everyone was drinking. It got really stupid. Everyone except me was talking tough. One of the guys started messing with me, and at first, Miguel stood up for me. But things got really twisted. He started telling me how ashamed he was of me because I was so soft. I started crying, which made him more angry. He said if I didn't stop, he'd make me. He jumped on me, started slapping my face, and kept yelling for me to stop. But it made it only worse. Then he started choking me. He had one hand over my mouth and his other around my throat.

"I started to pass out, and two of the guys pulled him off me. I just lay there trying to catch my breath, and one of the girls brought me some water. Finally, when I was able to, I stood up. The other guys were still holding him, but there was no need to. I told him I was soft like our mother but like her, I was strong in ways he could never understand. And I said he was mean and cruel and weak like our father. And that was why I was crying. I called him a no-good jackal and said he'd become like those men who raped our sister in the desert and left us for dead. When I left, I told him he was no brother of mine and flipped him off."

"I'm sorry to hear of that, Rafael. I can only guess how hard it was and has been. Miguel is not just your only remaining family, apart from your sister. He's your twin."

"No," Rafael said firmly. "I have many in my family. My people. It is to them I fled to Arizona."

"Did you and Miguel ever speak again?"

Rafael jumped down off the rock and began pacing back and forth across the dirt trail. "Speak? No. He texted me the day after the party and said how sorry he was. I didn't reply, so he tried calling me. I wouldn't take his calls. But after a few weeks with my people, I texted him and said I was okay and it was okay, but I would need time away. We've stayed in touch over the years by texting, but that's been it."

Rafael stopped his pacing, turned, and faced Daniel. "Padre, I never got past my anger toward him, and it was that anger I carried with me when I went to see him. As soon as he opened the door to his apartment, I exploded. I felt like a volcano erupting. I ripped him a new one. He was very defensive when I started on him. Whenever he'd try to say something, I felt like more lava was flowing."

He took a deep breath. "It's funny. When I think of it, I think I was talking to him like our *madre* did when she got mad at him, which was many times. And he felt it."

Daniel felt his phone vibrate, pulled it from his pocket, and read the text message. He arched his eyebrow and made a quick reply before turning his attention back to Rafael.

"Did you talk to him about getting into trouble?"

"I did. He asked how I found out, so I told him you told me when I went to visit you. He said he was sorry for beating up his boyfriend and was taking an anger management class. I don't think it will help because he has so much pain and anger. I asked him if he was thinking of killing himself, and he started laughing. He said it was stupid to think that."

"What about you? Do you think he might one day take his life?"

Rafael nodded several times. "I do. It scares me, Padre. I know what it's like. I heard about one of my friends who went to a regular Catholic school. When he came out to his parents, they were okay with it, but when he told his priest, the priest said he'd go to hell if he didn't change his ways. One night, he drowned himself. It really shook me, and that's when I decided I'd had enough of the Church. I'll never go back to it, Padre. It scares me to think Miguel might do the same thing. I don't know how I would go on without my brother, *mi hermano.* Now when I think about telling him he was no brother of mine, I really regret it."

"Rafael, everyone says stuff they shouldn't, especially to those they love most. Good people recognize it and come to regret saying it. Really good people then ask forgiveness from the person they hurt."

Rafael got quiet for a minute then said, "I guess that makes me a good person, but not a very good one. Maybe I'm a hypocrite because I do regret it, but I'm also glad I said what I did."

"Why?"

"When I said it, I wanted to hurt him, and that was the only way I could. But now, I think it's because I want him to know how stupid he was and how much he means to me, if that makes sense."

"It does. Maybe the next time you talk, you can tell him that. And tell him the scar of that confrontation remains. You see, Rafael, it's important to forgive, but it's very human not to forget. So we have to move past stuff like that or else we begin to feel sorry for ourselves and play the victim."

Rafael nodded. "I see. Thanks, Padre, that really helps. Miguel and I have a lot of talking to do. But, Padre, he's my brother and the person I love most."

"Well, as you've said before, you went through hell together. And when two people make their way through such a hell, it binds them in a way no other experience can."

"Is there a hell, Padre?"

"What do you think?"

Rafael shook his head. "Nah. I think they made that up just to scare people and get them to obey their rules. I believe in the Great Spirit and the thunder gods."

"That's a good belief system, Rafael."

Rafael's phone chimed. He looked at it and then at Daniel. "It's from Miguel. Says he just left his therapist's office and is heading home. He wants to know if you and I talked and if you would be willing to meet with him. What should I tell him, Padre?"

Daniel felt flummoxed. Talking with Rafael was one thing, but talking with Miguel was quite another. He wasn't sure if he had the mental or emotional capacity to do so just yet. He shrugged his shoulders.

"It's okay, Padre. I'll tell him we're still talking, which we are, and that I will head over to his place after we're done, which I will."

After Rafael sent his text, he and Daniel headed down to the parking lot. Neither said anything. When they got to their vehicles, Daniel spoke.

"After all you have been through, Rafael, I don't know how you find the strength and courage to go on as you do."

Rafael smiled widely as he opened the driver side door. "I do, Padre. *Mi madre, mi gente,* and *luna, mi abuela* in the sky. She's moving toward her full phase, so will start getting brighter tonight. It should rise right about there," he said pointing to the southeast horizon. "I think I might bring

Miguel up here. Maybe our grandmother's light can help us both begin to heal. How's that for a twist of fate? My twin tried to kill me, and here I am doing all I can to save him. Go figure."

14

JONATHAN PATTED THE soil around the rose of Sharon shrub he'd just planted. It was his second attempt at growing the shrub. The first one didn't come back after a late summer freeze killed off the plant. Such were the vagaries of gardening more than a mile and a half above sea level.

He smiled thinking of the two that grew in the Slovanco backyard when he was a boy. There was something gorgeous and intriguing about the shrub's flowers, how they opened into rich, vibrant pink, white, and red blooms. For some inexplicable reason, he used to pretend the flowers were fish when in their curled state. He yearned to return to those days of innocence. Then his imagination ran away with him like flights of childhood fantasies that rose out of the clouds of innocence. But he was far removed from the state of innocence, and his imagination often strayed into unblissful realms of late.

He stood and surveyed the scene. Despite the late arrival of spring in the high country, it was pleasing to see how beautifully rich his Zen garden was coming into bloom. There was still lots of work—playing in the mud, he called it—to do. The beauty of it was that he could immerse himself in it seven days a week. It felt good to be retired. He knew he would miss the classroom, but in his heart he knew he would always be a teacher and would find a way to express that essential part of his being. That life was now part of the ages.

Now in his sixties, he still felt strong and energetic. Far from moving to the sidelines of life, he felt the desire to participate in it as fully as his body would allow. As for his mind, there was no problem with it. He felt as sharp as ever intellectually. He placed his hands on his behind and bent backward, stretching his shoulders and pecs. Then he bent forward, allowing his arms to dangle and the nape of his neck to stretch. Finally he stood and stretched his arms skyward. It all felt very good.

After putting his garden tools and other material in the shed, Jonathan settled into a chair on the stone patio. He checked his phone for the time while he sipped iced tea from his water bottle. It was shortly after three. Daniel wouldn't arrive for another two hours or so, so he had plenty of time to relax, shower, and dress and do somersaults in his mind about how that conversation would go. Overthinking something, anticipating the worst, and letting his imagination run away with him were hazards for him. But he had good cause this time. Daniel had been growing more distant and even secretive over the past several months, more so than he had been over the past few years.

His distancing had begun slowly. Jonathan tried giving Daniel space, but recently the crack or fissure had been growing into a chasm. On the surface, they maintained the veneer of a relationship, but in practice it was crumbling. And Jonathan felt helpless. He swigged down the last gulps of the iced tea and decided to shower and dress. And maybe pour himself a Scotch afterward. He checked the time again. By the time he would have his drink, it would be happy hour. That was a good reason to be happy, he supposed.

Daniel took a deep breath as he drove up the entry ramp onto I-70. He'd be at Jonathan's in about thirty minutes. It was time. No more skirting around the issue. But he wondered if he would be able to find the right words and say them in the right tone. For all his oratorical skills, when it came to conversations that were very personal and could only be spoken from his personal point of view, he became flustered. But they needed to talk, and the truth had to be conveyed. He was who he was and it was long past time that he be true to his nature. He loved all he had and was grateful for his blessings and good fortune. He loved teaching. He loved—most times—being a Jesuit priest. He loved his living situation with James, Richard, and Maggie. He loved that he was in good health and free, he hoped, of any debilitating diseases. He loved how others respected him and how some, like Rafael, looked up to him for guidance and support. He loved living in the Denver metro area with its cultural and natural richness. He loved so much. And most of all, he loved Jonathan. And it was Jonathan he would hurt. Daniel hated that.

Daniel exited the highway, drove through town, and parked in front of Jonathan's home. When he got out, he stood at the bottom of the driveway, taking in the scene. The house had been in sore need of TLC when Jonathan had bought it fifteen or more years earlier. It was amazing to see the transformation Jonathan had brought to it. Gradually, he'd transformed it from dilapidated to a place of rich character. He texted Jonathan that he had arrived, and Jonathan replied saying he was out back and for him to come there.

"My friend," Jonathan said as Daniel appeared. "Welcome."

They embraced, clutching each other tightly for a few moments. After they pulled back, Jonathan motioned toward the other patio chair.

"I just poured myself a Scotch," he said. He pointed to a glass, bottle of Scotch, and container of ice. "Care for one?"

Daniel hesitated and then chuckled. "You know, you're the only one who can blend Buddhism with Scotch. It's the most interesting twist to ecumenism I have seen. Sure, I'll have one."

Jonathan dropped a few ice cubes in the glass, poured a splash over it, and handed the glass to Daniel. He raised his glass for a toast and they clinked glasses.

"The Buddha talked a lot about right living," Jonathan said. "For me, good Scotch is a part of that."

"Strange theology," Daniel replied. "Or would it be better to say *philosophy* since you don't see Buddhism as a religion."

"No, I don't. For me, it's a philosophy of life. As you know, I don't much care for religions. Yours is filled with rules, mostly about what not to do. Thou shalt not do this, that, or the next thing. I prefer the Buddha's spiritual directive: Just do the right thing."

"Yes, but what is the right thing?"

"You know, I know, everyone other than a madman knows what right living entails. Even the most ethically bankrupt amoralists know what is right. They just say they're above the rules and that moral and ethical behavior norms don't apply to them." He shook his head. "Daniel, we don't need a list of prescriptions and proscriptions about how to treat each other. We just need to listen to our inner promptings."

He sipped his drink and raised his glass, as if saluting the Buddha or punctuating what he'd just said. "Look. Theology is nothing more than an expenditure of brain power in a hopeless pursuit. It's a quest to find answers to questions that have already been answered in the minds of the pursuers. Rather than be curious and open to answers that might upset the apple cart of their position, theocrats close off anything that could negate their beliefs. For all the divisions among the dogmatic religions and within the religions themselves, it's merely a matter of them fine-tuning their preconceived—a priori—belief systems."

"I suppose I could respond and refute your contention, but I didn't come here to debate. Theology is not what I want to talk about now."

Jonathan nodded. "No, it's not. I suppose it's time for the conversation I've been dreading for thirty years." He raised an eyebrow. "But you know, Daniel, our conversations are not only about the nature of theology itself and its comparison to mythology and philosophy. They're about our nature, our being you and me. The way I see it is that you and I are of one spirit at war with itself. I manifest a certain aspect of that spirit energy; you an opposing one. Maybe that's why we've been good for each other over the years." Jonathan paused and focused on Daniel's eyes. "But my intuition tells me that is ending or is at least fracturing and heading toward a breaking point."

Daniel took a deep breath and a swig of his drink. He shook his head. "How do you always seem to know what's ruminating in my thoughts?"

"Because, Daniel, my love, I am you and you are me. A major difference between us is I know that and you will likely never know or grasp it. But what I don't know and need to come to understand is the why. On that, I'm lost."

"Jonathan, I don't know if I know the reasons for it. The best I can say is that there are multiple reasons, and you're not one of them. By you, I mean you as a person. Right now, it's the confines of our relationship that I've been finding restrictive. That I can put my finger on. You're right about us being of one spirit, and no matter what happens, I suspect that will not change. Since we found each other on that whale boat way back when, we've balanced each other."

"Balance is one way to describe our relationship," Jonathan replied, "but I think there is something more fundamental to it. We complete each other. We bring differing elements to it. That was a point I was getting at when I talked about the opposing natures of theology—which is you—and mythology—which is me. You believe in one God. I believe in many. But in the end, I believe that my many gods and each of us are one. Which always prompts the question in my mind about there being one God.

"Daniel, as you said, we balance each other, and as I said, we also complete each other. They're not the same, but they correlate. Both are necessary for a relationship to thrive. On the spiritual plane, it's evident how we complement each other. And we demonstrate that with the more mundane aspects of life, like how I live as kind of a mountain man who enjoys hiking, skiing, and puttering in my garden and you live as a city boy loving the scenes, noise, and congestion the urban area brings. They're how we each get our Zen. A fun part is how we enjoy foraying into each other's territory, literally and figuratively, but not staying too long."

Daniel turned his head and scanned Jonathan's Zen garden. He thought about what it had looked like years before when Jonathan first moved in. He found the transformation, like that of the house, inspirational. Jonathan said nothing as Daniel felt and absorbed the place's energetic emanations.

"I get your point," Daniel said. "I go into a church and you come out here. The deeper sense of that dichotomy has just struck me. It's not only about the where, a building versus a place in nature. It's also the act. I go into a closed space to pray and you go out to meditate. The inferences of that are profound: closed and restrictive versus open and free. And that gets to the nub of our relationship. I've always felt hindered, restricted, and confined, and you don't seem to be. In fact, I wonder if you find freedom within it."

Jonathan smiled widely and nodded. "Ah, as Falstaff said, 'Therein lies the rub.' You are correct. I feel free because I *am* free. You feel trapped because you are not free. I don't identify with my feelings; you do. I'm not this or that. I am that I am, to quote your God." He paused and stared into Daniel's eyes, holding his gaze for a moment. "Let's step out of the philosophical plane and into the real and cut to the chase. Is there another guy? Have you found another soul mate?"

Daniel took a deep breath. "No to both. I have not found another soul mate. I have one already, and that, I suspect, will never change." He paused, closed his eyes, and became pensive for a moment. Then he inhaled deeply again and looked directly at Jonathan. "It's long past time for me to be completely honest with you, Jonathan. The truth is, I have not only been unfaithful to my vow of chastity, I've been unfaithful to you. I haven't found one other guy. I've found several."

Jonathan stiffened and widened his eyes. "Several?"

Daniel nodded. "Over the last couple of years, I've met several and struck up relationships with a few. None of them lasting. But they taught me something. Opened my eyes to an aspect of me I knew to be true but refused to consciously acknowledge. Jonathan, I wonder if I'm polyamorous. I love being with men who are not priests, who have interests other than religion. Men who have all kinds of different personalities and do ordinary everyday stuff like going to work and having a drink afterward and watching a game. Or have their own place, a house or apartment they invite friends to, and neighbors they chat with or even fight with."

"So you sleep around?" Jonathan asked.

"No!" Daniel replied. "I don't sleep around. Most of the guys I've connected with I haven't had sex with. I admit to having sex with a few. A couple of those were fulfilling but none of them long-lasting. The others were flat—one night, sometimes one hour—stands. But each experience and all of them collectively have been helping me open my eyes to something I've put away and denied since I was a young man. While I love being a Jesuit and a priest, I miss not being just an ordinary gay man busy trying to save himself more than trying to save everyone else who comes and lays their crap at his doorstep."

He paused and sipped his drink to let what he'd just said sink in before continuing. "I have always felt like a tornado trapped in a bottle, spinning turbulently, constantly increasing the pressure of the container that I know will explode and shatter into pieces if I don't unscrew the lid and allow it—*me*—to escape." He looked at Jonathan straight in the eye. "And our relationship has become part of that whirlwind."

Both became quiet. The visual imagery of a whirlwind trapped in a container was an intense metaphor, and Daniel knew it would impact Jonathan deeply, allowing him to better understand the turmoil Daniel was not only currently feeling but had been feeling for decades, including all the years he and Jonathan had been together.

A mosquito landed on Jonathan's arm and he swatted it. "Daniel, when I was waiting for you to get here, I felt my anxiety growing. My intuition told me our talk would be a come-to-Jesus moment—or would it be better to say a come-to-Jesuit one?" He smiled weakly. "And a few moments ago when you told me about your dalliances, I admit to feeling hurt and angry. For an instant, I was ready to explode on you because I've been completely monogamous all these years. Have I been tempted? Yes, more than once. But it was you I wanted to remain with even if it meant not being able to lead what you called an ordinary everyday life.

"I could go on about why, but maybe it's better to put that off for another time. All that said, the truth now is that my heart aches for you. For the first time, I can see your inner turmoil. I'm now seeing why our relationship has been fracturing. You haven't been leading a double life. I now see you've been leading a triple one."

He drained the last of his drink, slid forward on his chair, and placed his hand on Daniel's knee. "My heart aches for you, but it's aching for me too. I'm feeling hurt by what you've told me, but I'm also feeling grateful that you did. That says something about me. I had thought I could read you and that I knew you better than you knew yourself. It seems now that I did not. Perhaps it was because I chose to live an illusion. It looks like you're not the only one who needs to do some deep soul-searching."

He waved at another mosquito and stood up. "The bugs are starting to bite. Let's go inside."

He picked up the bottle of Scotch and Daniel grabbed the ice bucket. They slowly made their way around to the back door. As they walked into the house, Daniel inhaled deeply.

"I smell lasagna."

"Your favorite despite being Irish to the bone. You must have a recessive gene."

They continued their discussion over dinner.

"The love I have felt for you over the years has not only not diminished, it has grown deeper," Daniel admitted. "I cannot imagine where I'd be if we hadn't met."

"I know it will take time for me to ingest and decipher what you've revealed, Daniel, but that is my issue. Thank you for speaking so forthrightly. How I feel for you hasn't and won't change. But I understand your need to follow your path. You have to be true to yourself. So from my end, let me be the one to twist the lid off the container of our relationship. Your spirit is free to fly wherever it will."

"Thank you," Daniel said as the two toasted freedom of spirit.

They ate without speaking, and Daniel filled his plate with a second helping.

"Daniel, when I ask this, it's not to be spiteful or cruel," Jonathan said at last. "But I know you, and my intuition also tells me there's something you've held back on telling me. Something very personal. That needs to be said to completely clear the air."

Daniel stiffened.

"What's his name?"

Daniel hesitated before replying. "Mason."

"Do you love him?"

Daniel pushed his plate away, rested his forearms on the table, and leaned forward. "I'm not sure what I feel. He's a bit strange in his own way. But then, aren't we all?"

"True enough," Jonathan said. "Time for some music."

While Daniel cleared the table and cleaned up the kitchen, Jonathan logged on to his computer and opened Pandora.

"What are you in the mood for listening to?" he asked.

"Something soft and soothing."

"Me too. Judy Collins and company it is." The strains of "Both Sides Now" soon wafted across the room.

Jonathan was already seated in the single chair lightly singing along with Judy when Daniel joined him in the sitting room, where the lights had been lowered and candles lit.

"You know it's one of my favorite songs," Jonathan said when it finished. "Poignant. I especially love the last stanza where she sings about how old friends are acting strange and saying she's changed."

Daniel closed his eyes, sat quietly, and let the songs gently massage his heart. Thoughts of what was said echoed through his mind. When he opened them, he saw that Jonathan had closed his eyes and seemed to be enraptured by the music too. The cover of Rod MacIver's *The Heron Dance Book of Love and Gratitude* lying on the coffee table caught his eye. It had been lying there for years but he had never picked it up and read from it. He began leafing through it. A passage from Henry Miller's *Reflections* about trust in everything that happens, even the painful things, made him pause and reread it a couple of times.

He glanced up at Jonathan, who still sat with his eyes closed, and thought of the pain he had inflicted. He scrolled through a few more pages and saw a passage from Katherine Hepburn, one of his and Jonathan's favorite actresses. He imagined her delivering the lines in her throaty voice about love having nothing to do with what you're expecting but rather being only about giving. And if lucky, you might get love in return.

Daniel closed the book and studied the grayish-purple watercolor scene Rod had painted of two herons. One was afloat on water and the other was spreading its wings and lifting off in flight. The symbolism was striking. He pulled the book up his chest, folded it into an embrace, and wondered about his capacity for love.

15

THE SMELL OF freshly baked bread awakened Daniel. He peered at the clock on the nightstand, and when he saw it was almost seven, he pulled his head back under the sheet and tried to block out the world. To no success. He could hear strains of music softly sifting through the slightly ajar door. When he pulled the sheet back from his head and looked at the room through slitted eyes, it took a few seconds to focus his mind on what he was seeing. But it finally dawned on him that the reason he didn't recognize the room was that he had never before slept in it. It was the guest room. Up until last night, whenever he stayed overnight, he had always shared Jonathan's bed.

Daniel rolled onto his back. He was groggy and exhausted, but at least he'd gotten a few hours of sleep. After tossing and turning much of the night, he'd finally fallen into a fitful sleep sometime after three in the morning. Disturbing dreams had once again commandeered his sleep. It was an ongoing struggle that was increasingly exerting control over him. He struggled to fall asleep in the first place, and when he did, all kinds of bizarre dreams flooded the landscape of his dream world. Many were incongruent with characters from his daily life in all kinds of inane situations, but others were longer, deeper, and at times, chilling.

He swung his legs to the side of the bed, stood, and made his way down to the bath to wash up. When he looked in the mirror, the image reflected back at him was grotesque and disheveled. After washing his face, Daniel rubbed the towel against his two-day-old beard. He thought of the beard he'd grown when he visited Vincente. When he returned home, he decided to shave it off and was glad to be rid of it. One reason was that it required grooming and regular maintenance. A daily shave was easier. The other reason he'd shaved it off was that it wasn't him. A beard gave him a look that seemed to him incongruent with his character. He ran a brush through his thick hair and realized he needed a haircut. Once slightly graying with a salt-and-pepper appearance, it now looked more like dirty snow. When he finished getting himself together and left the room, he thought about the fact he was now a guest in Jonathan's home.

Jonathan was in the kitchen preparing breakfast, and when Daniel croaked a good morning to him, Jonathan turned and gave him an appraising look before saying, "You look like crap."

"I feel like crap," Daniel said as he climbed onto a stool at the breakfast bar.

Jonathan nodded slightly. "Tea or coffee?"

"Coffee. I need something to jar me."

"It'll take a few minutes. I put it together in case you wanted it but decided to wait until you got up." He flipped on the brewer, took a sip of his tea, and returned to his task of slicing strawberries for a breakfast fruit salad. "I take it you didn't sleep well."

"I hardly slept at all. I kept tossing and turning through the night. Then when I fell asleep, it wasn't good."

The aroma of coffee brewing began to fill the air. Jonathan set the two bowls with chopped and sliced fruit at their places at the breakfast bar and began prepping the eggs. The gentle sounds of Enya's voice and the aroma of freshly brewed coffee and frying bacon softened and warmed the silence.

After he had everything prepared, Jonathan set it out and settled onto the stool next to Daniel. "Dig in," he urged Daniel. "It'll help you feel better."

"I feel guilty," Daniel said as he filled his plate.

"About?"

"I come up here, deliver some difficult, unwanted news, and here you are treating me like royalty. I don't get it."

As he spread preserves on his toast, Jonathan raised his eyes and asked, "You don't? After how many years?"

"Look. I know how reserved and emotionally disciplined you can be, but still. If you had told me you wanted out of our relationship, I probably would've had a meltdown."

"Yes, you would have. But that's you, not me. It's your nature. Don't forget. You're a Leo fire, and I'm an Aquarius air."

"So I'm hot and you're cold?"

"Something like that. But it's more than that, Daniel. You see what's in front of you. I see that, but I also see what's hidden behind, beyond, or below what's on the surface. I operate from the mind and see with my third eye. You see with your visual cortex and heart. That's not bad. It's one of the reasons we've been good for each other and will continue to be no matter how this turns out. You need air to survive. I need fire to warm me. If you get enraged, you can snuff me out. But then you would die. I can inflame you with my gusts, which I believe I have a few times over the years."

"Yes, you have," Daniel admitted as he poured himself a second cup of coffee. "I get that, or at least understand your point even if I don't agree with it. But still, you act as if our separating is not an issue, not a big deal."

"Well, my love, I assure you it *is* a big deal. The tremors from it are near the max on my personal Richter scale. Does it hurt? Yes. Am I now out of balance? Sure. Am I anxious about what's next? You bet I am. But you know what? Those hurts are no more than feelings, and I control my feelings, not the other way around. Sometimes they get the upper hand, but I work to rein them back under control. Only one of us can be in charge. Me or them.

"I've come to understand that emotional pain is no different than physical pain. Both can cause great discomfort to the point that you can't sleep, and they're both signals that something is wrong. That's crucial to always keep in mind about pain, whether physical or emotional. One major difference between the two pains is that aspirin won't alleviate or make emotional pain go away. You can't take two after your heart is broken and wake up in the morning feeling better. And that makes sense. Aspirin is a substance and so is the body and nervous system. Heartache is nonphysical but just as real. So I do other stuff to ease it."

"Like what?" Daniel asked as he reached for another slice of toast.

"Like detaching for one. I could get all pissed off with you and throw a tantrum or play the victim and cry. But to what end? If anything, stuff like that only makes things worse. Another approach begins with detaching. It's something I'm working on—detaching from the emotion so I can explore the why and what brought us to this point without becoming awash in emotion about it. And when I say us, I'm not just meaning our relationship. I also mean us as individuals. So I wonder if I've done anything that brought this about or contributed to it. Or if I haven't done enough. And I need to work to understand this from your end. Could the potential demise of our relationship be the result of something within it or is there another factor that has entered the picture?"

He shook his head. "I don't know, Daniel, I don't know. And that calculus is what is eating at me most."

"Calculus. You make it sound like a mathematical equation. Well, I'm not the sum of my parts. And neither are you."

"You're right. We're not equations that can be solved. We're complex beings. Still, it's imperative for me to understand, not just to feel. And until I do, I will keep my emotions in check." He took a sip of his tea before adding. "And probably forever after."

Daniel poured himself a third cup and glanced over at Jonathan, who sat expressionless sipping his tea.

"Mind if I make more toast?" Daniel asked.

"Help yourself. I have another loaf in the freezer. Oh, open the oven. There's another tray of bacon. I know how much of a carnivore you are, so I fried up the whole pound."

Daniel smiled. "Thank you. You know, I'm getting my appetite back. I might make a bacon sandwich."

"Go for it."

"I wish I could be more like you," Daniel said as he slid back onto the stool with his bacon on toast sandwich. "What's the word I'm looking for? Ah, yes, cerebral. Deliberate. You think stuff through before reacting."

"I'd say more like process and internalize the information rather than think stuff through. There's a difference. Thinking is a conscious act. Internalizing something and letting it percolate allows the psyche to process it without interference from the conscious mind that is constantly asking what if and debating pros and cons. Still, what I do is not always good. Sometimes you have to act immediately, like when a careening car is heading toward you. You don't have time to debate the pros and cons about which way to jump or run. And honestly, I wish I could be more like you at times. Passionate. Zealous. But the truth is, if everyone were like me, this would be a pretty boring world. And if everyone were like you, we'd have killed ourselves off eons ago."

"I agree with you on that. It's just …" Daniel paused. What seemed like a clear point to make had instantly evaporated.

Jonathan waited a few moments, but when Daniel shook his head and shrugged, he spoke.

"Daniel, once upon a time, as you recall, I was very much where you are. Then something happened. Rather, I did something that changed all that. I slit my wrist when I was in a stupor. You remember it well because you were the one who found me and saved my life. I'd hit rock bottom. I didn't realize it then. I was focused on recovering. Then, one day I literally woke up and realized I had not only left my previous life and all its baggage behind, I had entered a whole new universe. What was once nearly always an either-or dichotomous world of right and wrong and good and evil had changed into a multiplex world. It's that duality you continue to operate in, and it's guided and promulgated by your faith. And as long as you stay mired in that two-sided paradigm of sin and forgiveness, you will struggle."

He set his left hand atop Daniel's right.

"Because what and who seems bad is not always bad. In fact, what or who seems bad on the surface can be more good than what or who seems good. You might recall that it's one of the themes of John Steinbeck's *East of Eden*. Cal, who personified Cain, ironically, or perhaps not so ironically, turned out in the end to be the noble son. Despite the harm and hurt he caused, Cal was the one who stayed with and took care of his father, who had treated him pretty harshly throughout his life. Aron, the personification of Abel, collapsed and fled. He couldn't bear the truth about their mother."

Jonathan went to make a fresh cup of tea and continued talking as he heated the water. "As I said earlier, I look for and often find what is beyond, behind, or underneath." When he returned to his seat, Daniel was mutely staring into his cup. "What's wrong?" he asked.

Daniel looked up with a start. "Oh, nothing wrong. It's just that something you said made something click in my mind. Something I couldn't put my finger on, but I think I can now."

"What's that?"

"It's not a what, but a who."

The Sunday afternoon traffic back to Denver from the mountains was its usual summertime congestion. Being in no hurry and to avoid the helter-skelter pace in the passing lane, Daniel stayed in the right lane, content to be lost in his thoughts. Suddenly, a car sped by, and the suddenness jarred him. A moment later, he heard its tires screeching as it swerved and skidded sideways trying to avoid crashing into the stopped vehicles ahead of it. It crashed into the median and then ricocheted, resulting in a multivehicle pileup.

Traffic came to a halt. Daniel turned off the ignition, jumped out, and raced to the scene of the accident. Others from vehicles ahead of him had already begun to help the victims. Daniel turned his attention to a vehicle that had been spun sideways. Its front end was wedged against the guardrail. In it, he saw two women. The younger one, the driver, stared straight ahead, seemingly in shock. The other in the passenger seat was an older woman whose head was slumped forward. He tapped hard on the driver's window and tried to open the door. It was locked and the woman wasn't responding.

"Are you okay?" he yelled as he banged on the window.

The woman turned slightly, then full on. She shook her head. Her face was ashen. Another Good Samaritan tried opening the passenger side door, but it too was locked. "We can help," he yelled, "but you need to unlock the doors or lower your window."

The younger woman shook her head a couple of times, apparently trying to clear the fog, and turned toward her passenger. "Mother!" she screamed. "Mother!"

She fiddled with the door handle and finally opened it a bit. Daniel grabbed it and swung it full wide.

"Can you get out?" he asked. "Stand?"

She nodded. "Yes! But please help my mother. She's not moving."

A woman came up behind Daniel. "Let me help her," she said. "You help that guy on the other side."

Daniel ran around to the passenger side where the man had managed to release the woman's seat belt. When he did, she slumped into his arms.

"She's unconscious, but I think she's still breathing," he said.

With Daniel's help, he eased the woman out. They laid her on a blanket someone had spread out on the asphalt. The man lifted her head and slid a rolled up jacket that was handed to him under it.

Daniel knelt down, put his ear to her nose, and nodded. "She's beathing but barely. Very shallow. She needs help immediately." He set his left hand on her forehead and made the sign of the cross with his right. With it, the woman took a bit of a deeper breath. No sooner had he finished than he felt an arm grab his shoulder.

"We got this, sir," an EMT said. "Please stand back."

She quickly pulled Daniel to his feet and with another EMT, she began administering first aid. Daniel watched in stunned silence as the two EMTs efficiently worked, trying to save the woman's life. He looked around at the quiet faces intently watching. Sirens pierced the air and bright emergency lights flashed ahead and around him. He stepped over to the guardrail, leaned against it, and wrapped his arms around himself, taking a deep breath.

A police officer approached him. "Sir, are you okay? Do you need some help?"

Daniel shook his head. "No, I'm fine. It's just the sudden shock of it all."

The man Daniel had helped to get the woman out of the car came over. "You a priest?"

Daniel nodded.

"I used to be Catholic," the man said, "but no longer am. I still believe. I just don't know what I believe. I'm glad you were there to bless her. It might've saved her life."

Daniel stared at the man trying to process the enormity of what he'd just said.

"Thank you, Father," the man said as he turned to go.

A moment later, Daniel realized he hadn't replied to the man to thank him for his words. He immediately stepped back over to the scene and scoured the faces of the onlookers, but he couldn't spot the man. He saw the EMTs sliding the stretcher with the woman on it into the ambulance as her daughter watched with tears streaming down her face. Daniel wandered through the mayhem, still trying to spot the man who'd spoken to him, but he was nowhere to be seen. It was curious. It was as if the man had disappeared. He saw cars ahead slowly inching forward. Apparently, the police, with the help of a couple of tow trucks, had cleared a lane to allow the traffic to ease by the scene. He quickly ran back to his vehicle, started it up, and joined the procession slowly moving through the carnage.

When he got back to the rectory, he let himself in through the back door. Maggie looked up from her work and stared for a moment. "Father, you look like you've seen a ghost."

"I might've, Maggie. I think I might've."

Daniel went to his room, and after showering and shaving, lay on his bed. He crossed his arms over his chest and breathed slowly and deeply. With each breath, he could feel his body relax and succumb to the weariness that pervaded him. He pictured scenes from the accident: the big picture of the scene and then smaller ones of the older woman and her daughter; the man he had assisted who'd thanked him for administering a blessing to the woman as she lay on the ground. He sent another blessing to all the victims and offered a prayer that all would survive and recover.

Then he breathed deeply and felt his left arm drift to his side while his right arm sat above his heart on his chest.

> The scene was a placid, bucolic open meadow. The sun shone lazily and warmly. Only a slight breeze riffled the air. Suddenly on the horizon, Daniel saw a large beast charging down at him. After a moment's hesitation, he turned and ran toward a split rail fence. He climbed over it, glanced briefly back at the beast, and ran down the trail through the woods.
>
> When he rounded a curve on the trail, he saw the animal, the size of a large bison, charging him again from in front of him. He fled into the woods, plowing through the brush and dodging trees, but he could hear the animal's pounding hooves growing nearer.
>
> At last he came out onto an empty paved street in a community. He looked over his shoulder and saw the beast charging at him from between two houses and ran to the front door of the nearest house. It was unlocked, so he quickly let himself in and slammed the door behind him. A young girl appeared and asked if he was okay. She didn't seem to be upset that he had broken into her home. He shouted that there was a large animal chasing him and it was just outside, but she didn't seem to care. He could hear the animal's

bellows, and when he peered through the narrow window panes that framed the door, he saw a large bison snout pressed up against it and heard it stomping and snorting. He stood back, first frozen in terror but then in awe.

Daniel's eyes popped open. He was panting and his heart was racing. He lay there taking in deep breaths as he visualized images from the dream. After a few minutes, he got up, went to his desk, opened his journal, and wrote an entry detailing the dream. After rereading it and touching it up, he leaned back in his chair and whispered to himself, "Good Lord, what's happening to me?"

16

SOPHIA'S OFFICE WAS nondescript. In Daniel's mind, it belied her prominence as a renowned Jungian psychotherapist. He was struck not only by its location but also by its simplicity. It contrasted completely with what he had imagined it would look like when Sophia told him she had an office in Colorado. He had pictured a spacious office with a large, hand carved desk topped with neatly arranged letter trays, books, and framed photos of Vincente and memorable landscapes. He had pictured a leather desk chair with comfortable seats on the other side of the desk, plush carpeting, and expensive paintings hanging on paneled walls.

Instead, the room was only about ten by twelve feet and located in an early twentieth century brownish-red brick building in an older established Denver neighborhood. One print of a lily pond hung on a beige wall. The furniture consisted of two chairs upholstered in a somewhat worn red fabric, a print fabric love seat, a pole lamp, a medium-sized wooden table and chair, both in need of refinishing, that sat in the corner.

Sophia had texted apologetically that she was stuck in traffic on I-25 and for Daniel to let himself in and get comfortable.

Daniel retrieved his notepad and pen from his pack, scanned his notes, and jotted a few additional notes in the margins. Thoughts ran through his mind about where to begin. It would be their first session, and since meeting Sophia in Santa Fe, much had happened that added to the swirling clouds of his mind.

"Good morning," Sophia said as she strode into the office. Daniel stood to greet her. "I'm not sure if an accident caused the backup or if it was just congestion. Please, get comfortable."

"Thank you," Daniel said as he sat back down. "I have extra time, so don't rush on my part."

"I appreciate that," Sophia said as she got herself organized. I have a meeting at eleven, but it's just down the hall and we rarely start on time anyway." She grabbed her pad and pen and sat. "Whew! Like my digs?"

"I do, but I have to say, I was surprised by them. I thought you said your office was in Littleton."

"My main office is, but I keep this smaller one for clients I believe would be more comfortable in a simpler setting. You're obviously one of them."

"I'll take that as a compliment."

She smiled. "It is, which should tell you something I sense about you."

"And that is?"

"You tell me. You know what it is."

Daniel nodded. "I'll think on it. Thank you for taking time to see me, Sophia. I have to admit that I am a bit nervous. This is the first time in many years I've talked formally to a professional therapist. And then it was to another priest. Apart from that experience, I'm usually the one hearing another confess."

"Do you think of our talk as a confession?"

"Good question. I'm not sure. Maybe it's because I'm a priest. But then I've had plenty of people, mostly students, open up outside the bounds of the confessional. Now that you mention it, it's interesting that I would put this within the context of confessing. Maybe I'm unconsciously thinking I've sinned and you're here to absolve me. But that's ridiculous."

"You said your use of the word *confession* might've come up from your unconscious. Let's talk about that. What do you mean by your unconscious?"

"Hmm … maybe the hidden part of my mind. Something residing in the back of my brain that stores memories of past experiences and habits."

"Is your mind, as you call it, part of your unconscious or is that unconscious state you referred to part of your mind?"

Daniel shrugged. "I don't know."

"That's a good answer, but before we get too far afield, let's talk about what's been happening in your life."

Daniel sat straighter and cleared his throat. "Let's see. I'll give you a quick overview. I've broken up with my longstanding partner, who deserved far better than the way I've been treating him. I've fallen under the spell of a man I neither can break free from nor want to. I'm seriously considering renouncing my vows and leaving the Jesuits and the priesthood. I've been requested to intervene with a troubled former student who beat up his boyfriend and whose twin brother came to see me out of the blue. The twin is also in a bad way, having gotten an HIV diagnosis. And what may be the worst is that my sleep has been minimal and often restless due to disturbing dreams."

He stopped, took a deep breath, and clenched his jaw. "Other than that," he said sarcastically, "life's good."

"That was quite a torrent," Sophia said calmly. "I could tell through your body language that you are carrying quite a load. Thank you for trusting me with it all. It cannot be easy."

She shifted in her seat. "Perhaps it might be best to take a few moments to allow yourself to become composed. So let's just sit quietly for a few minutes. Close your eyes and slow your breathing. Slow deep breaths in and slower exhalations." Daniel did so. "Now become aware of your body. Feel the chair you're sitting on. The brush of your sleeve against your arm as you move or twitch. Feel your feet inside your shoes resting on the floor. Take note of any other incoming sensations. Then focus inside. What are you feeling and where? Take as much time as you need. When you're ready, slowly open your eyes and nod to let me know you're ready to go on."

Daniel followed her instructions, and when he opened his eyes, he felt as if he'd just awakened from a nap. He slowly inhaled one more time and nodded.

Sophia continued. "Addressing everything you've told me collectively would be daunting, but if we address each separately, we should be able to get to the root of each issue, as well as see a relationship or pattern among them. What do you think?"

"It makes sense. But when I think of them like a laundry list, there's something that separates my dreams from the others. At least in my mind."

"What's that?"

"Control. Even though each of the other things I've mentioned seems out of control right now, I believe I can act to influence them. But I can't control the dreams. Instead, they control me."

"Why do you say they control you?"

"This might be a strange way of putting it, but they've now gotten into my head. I know that seems like an absurd statement in that, of course, they're in my head because that's where they originate. What I mean is that during my waking hours, I can't stop thinking about them. I'm afraid I'm becoming obsessed with them."

"That's interesting. But let's back up to something you just said. You said your dreams originate in your head. How do you know that?"

"Well, that's where my brain is."

"True, but does that then mean that's where your dreams are? All in your head? Could they be something outside your brain, even outside your literal body, something substantial that your brain is observing and processing just as it does with all other incoming sensory data and perceptions?"

"Something separate from me?"

"No, not *from* you. Think of them as being part of your psyche, not of your conscious mind but of your unconscious. When you think of the concept of the unconscious, what comes to mind?"

"It's a condition that one is in when they're not conscious."

"Okay, picture someone who is unconscious. Are they asleep or what?"

"I wouldn't say asleep. I'd say just not being consciously aware."

"Explain consciously aware."

"Not being able to take in information through the senses."

"Is a sleeping person able to take in or receive information?"

"I don't know for sure, but I imagine they can."

"So by your definition, when one is asleep, they are not unconscious. They are conscious but in a sort of limbo, neither fully conscious nor unconscious."

"I'd say so."

"Okay, let's operate from that premise. Tell me about one of the dreams you vividly recall."

Daniel took a deep breath and described the dream he had in which a grown man and two younger ones were secured to poles in a tepee and the shaman of the tribe performed a ritual during which he poured gourds of water over hot rocks, making the tepee a sweat lodge. When he finished describing the dream, he took a long swig from his water bottle.

"Just thinking about that scene makes me sweat," he said. "When I had that dream, it didn't make much sense. It still doesn't, although now I think I can associate the three characters with real people."

Sophia said nothing, so Daniel continued.

"I was the older man, and the two younger men were the two former students I mentioned earlier. They're twins, Rafael and Miguel. They were students of mine about twelve years ago. I mentioned them when I described the many issues I'm dealing with. As we talk, I'll tell you more about both since they've unexpectedly come back into my life and are having a major impact on it."

"What causes you to associate the three characters in your dream with you, Rafael, and Miguel?"

"For some strange reason, I'm sensing that the three of us seem to be connected. Our life courses seem to be intertwined. It's no coincidence that they, like me, are struggling with issues, and it's no coincidence that they have reappeared in my life. Years ago, when they came into my class, I was immediately impressed and taken by them. That wasn't unusual. Over the years, I had certain students who, for one reason or another, stood out. They were exceptions, and I mean that in a couple of ways. Talent wise, a few were exceptional. I had a sense that they would really stand out in their chosen fields and might one day be recognized for their achievements. Others were exceptional because of their personalities and life stories.

"Miguel and Rafael were exceptions in both senses. They'd managed to survive some horrific experiences as boys: the terror they faced in El Salvador, escaping to America with all the accompanying brutality that came with it, and trying to survive once they got here, all compounded by the tragedies that afflicted their family. And yet, they excelled—Miguel through the intellect and Rafael through art."

He paused in reflection before continuing. "For reasons only they can explain, they seemed to appreciate my classes. I could tell how they absorbed every idea and thought raised not only by me, but also by their fellow students. They were constantly engaged."

"Why do you think that was?"

"I can't be sure, of course, but I suspect it was because they knew—and forgive my language—how shitty life can be. There were terrible things in their lives, but they weren't going to allow their circumstances to prevent them from living their lives fully. They appreciated how fortunate they were despite their ordeals and wanted to make the best of that good fortune. Unlike some of their classmates, they were not about to squander away a priceless gift like education."

Daniel paused and drank some water before continuing.

"Seeing them graduate was one of the highlights of my career. But something told me they would not be leaving my life, that we would remain in contact. That wasn't unusual either. During his twenties, Rafael would reach out on occasion. He was forging his path and struggling but staying at it. But I never heard from Miguel directly. When we talked, Rafael would update me about what he knew, but it was as if Miguel had gone into another place, a darker place, if you will. Sadly, it seemed the brothers were growing distant from each other. I say sadly because they were all each other had. For all their growing and maturing years, they'd seemed to be inseparable. Yet they were separating, which I sensed would not bode well for them. They were joined, as we say, at the hip. Not just because they were twins, I think, but also because they had endured so much together.

"Then out of nowhere, I got that visit from Miguel's boyfriend. He told me Miguel had been arrested for assaulting him. He'd told the DA about Miguel's struggles, and the DA agreed to defer prosecution if Miguel got some counseling. The boyfriend was hoping I would be willing to talk with Miguel because he felt Miguel trusted me. And then Rafael resurfaced, bringing with him a very personal and complex story that included becoming HIV positive. Everything in their lives was blowing up, and somehow it circled back to me."

He paused and looked at Sophia intently. "I just don't see it all as coincidental. Given their history and my role in it, it just seems we were destined to be connected. That they hadn't shown up in my classroom by chance."

"Synchronicity?" Sophia asked.

"Yes. It confirms for me what Robert Hopcke wrote about there being no accidents. So when I look at that dream in hindsight, I can see the three characters being us. But I just can't make sense of it." He shook his head. "I don't know."

"Have you had other dreams of the three of you?"

"Not that I can recall with the three of us, but I did have one with Miguel. It was unnerving. I think maybe we were in his apartment, and I was watching him perform a self-sacrificing ritual. He was cutting himself across his abdomen, making a cross. It shook me. The one in which we were in a tepee tied to stakes wasn't unnerving, but that one was."

"Do you think they, the two dreams, relate or are connected to each other?"

"I think they are. In the first one, it was as if the three of us were joined together in some type of bond or union. A tribe perhaps. In the second, it was much more personal, but just with me and Miguel."

"Do you think the dream of him cutting himself and his troubles are related?"

"I sense they are, but I'm not sure how. In real life—or should I say, waking life—his destructive act was outwardly focused. In the dream, it was directed at himself. So they seem to be opposite forms of destruction."

"Could they not be opposite but, instead, one and the same?"

"I don't understand."

"I'm speculating, but the commonality between the conscious act and the unconscious one you dreamed about is hurt. The waking act is one of turning the hurt outward and the dream act is one of turning the hurt inward."

Daniel nodded. "Yes, I can see that."

Sophia continued. "In the first dream, you said it was as if the three of you were like members of a tribe. Could that association not be of a tribe, but of something much more personal?"

"Like what?"

"You tell me. What association do people have that is most personal?"

Daniel's eyes grew wide. He focused them onto Sophia.

"Family?"

Sophia smiled softly.

"Oh, my God," Daniel said softly. "They see me as their father, or at least as a father figure." He took a deep breath. "Whew. It makes sense. I haven't told you about the abuse their natural father inflicted on them. And before that, I suspect he wasn't affectionate with his sons." He paused for a moment. "I don't know why, but I can see that view of me as a father figure more readily with Rafael than Miguel." He shook his head. "I'm just not feeling that kind of relationship with Miguel. Maybe it's me and some sort of resistance, but I suspect he's not thinking of me in a father context. But let me think about it."

Sophia nodded. "But still, when you welcomed them unconditionally and gave them unconditional caring and support, they naturally could have put you in their father's stead, at least initially."

Daniel sat quietly reflecting on the insights. "Maybe." He glanced at the clock on the wall to his right, saw it was past his time, and began gathering his things together.

"Another related thought just came to mind, something I hadn't told you about either. When Miguel started getting into heavy stuff in our talks, issues I felt I was getting in over my head on, I got Vincente involved, and he began seeing Miguel. Maybe he saw that as a rejection on my part. Hmm. Maybe we can explore that more next time."

"Of course, but we'll need to keep the focus on you and anything else that comes to mind, especially if it relates to your dreams."

"Definitely," he replied as they both stood and he moved toward the door. "Like the one in which I'm in a lions' den. That one puzzles me."

"I can't wait to hear about it. Do you want to set a time to meet again?"

"Can I call or text you in a day or two? I have a few commitments I need to take care of, but I do want to see you again while you're in town."

"Absolutely. I'll check my calendar to be sure, but I believe I'll be here for about another week. And I promise next time I'll be on time."

Daniel made his way down the stairs and to his truck. He let it idle while his conversation with Sophia played through his mind. A clearer picture was starting to take shape, at least on part of his troubles. As he took his phone off airplane mode, he thought of Mason and remembered he'd agreed to water his plants and feed the fish, so he headed south on I-25 through the thick of Denver's late morning traffic.

17

DANIEL ENTERED THE access code to Mason's apartment on the key pad and eased the door open. Immediately the smell of coffee brewing struck him. Despite it being a bright, sunny day, the room was in shadow because the window coverings were closed. Surprised, he called Mason's name but got no answer. As he stepped into the front room, he saw Mason curled up on the sofa wrapped in his white terry cloth bathrobe. A cup of coffee sat on the coffee table next to an open family photo album. As Daniel looked down at him, debating whether he should rouse him, Mason opened his eyes.

"Good morning," he whispered. "Thanks for coming over."

"Are you sick?" Daniel asked in surprise.

"No. Just tired. Very tired."

Mason slowly pushed himself up into a seated position, leaned against the armrest, and curled his long legs beneath him. His hair was rumpled and his face looked drawn. His voice was low as he said, "Pour yourself a cup of coffee. You might need to nuke it because I put the pot on some time ago."

"Thanks, I'm good," Daniel replied as he lowered himself down onto the chair across the coffee table from Mason.

Daniel studied Mason's face in the dim light. "What's going on?"

Mason remained still with his arms wrapped around his chest and spoke without opening his eyes. “I was thinking about when I would pilot our boat out onto Lake Pontchartrain. That was a good time in my life.” He opened his eyes and smiled softly. “I like to think about that. You know I was married once, right?”

Daniel nodded.

“Her name was Camille. She was a beauty queen. She was two years younger than me and in the same class as my sister. My parents really liked her. Actually, what they liked was my marrying her so they could be part of her family. Her family had money. We weren’t poor by any stretch of the imagination, but what my parents wanted was status. And connecting to the right family would give them that. I hated that. I didn’t hate them, just what they stood for, what was important to them.

“My granny was very different. When I was little and got scared, she would sit with me and hold me. She’d tell me stories about when she grew up in the Great Depression and how times were really tough. When she was there and I woke up crying, she’d come in and sit with me. She never left the room until I fell back asleep. When she wasn’t there, my mother would come into my room and sit on my bed until I stopped crying. Then she’d leave and close the door behind her. I would lie there shaking under the covers. I don’t know why. I was just scared.”

He reached down for his coffee and cupped it in his hands.

"My father was a horrid man. All business. Everything had to be perfect. He was obsessed. He'd make me and my brother help him take care of the lawn. I hated it. But when I was fourteen, he bought a boat. He wasn't good at captaining it, but I was, so he started to treat me a little better and let me pilot it. I wanted to prove to him I could do it, that I was grown-up. I think what I really wanted to prove to him was that I was better at it than him." He smiled wryly. "That I was better than him."

"When's the last time you talked to him?" Daniel asked.

"We don't talk much anymore. He never calls me. I call him every once in a while to check on how Mom is doing. Camille and I had a loveless marriage. It was for show. After we divorced, I finally accepted the fact that I was gay. It scared me—not being gay, but telling everyone I was. I started with friends. A few were okay with it, but most weren't. Some were downright hostile and others were polite, but it wasn't long before I was no longer part of their life. When I told my parents, they disowned me for a few years. They said I was a child of Satan. I wasn't surprised. It was the only time I stood up to my dad. I told him that made him Beelzebub.

"You should see Camille now. I found her on Facebook. She must weigh two hundred pounds. At first I laughed, but after I thought about it, I felt sorry for her."

"Why?"

"Because she was just as much a victim of that culture as me. My sister told me Camille had a secret boyfriend in high school. He enlisted in the military—the Navy, I think it was—so he left town. I think they kept in touch over the years, and after he got out, they got back together and were having an affair. It didn't bother me. In fact, I was glad she found someone to give her what I couldn't. But I knew it wouldn't end well for them. His family had no money and hers would never accept him."

He shrugged his shoulders and sipped more coffee. "I hated that life. Everything except for being on that boat on Lake Pontchartrain." He sighed. "And it's not gotten much easier since. Did I tell you about Kendall?"

Daniel shook his head.

"I met him in Austin. I thought he was a great guy, so I moved in with him. I felt like everything was going well, and one day when I came home from work, all of my belongings were in trash bags on the apartment building lawn. He must've seen me from the window because he texted and said he changed the lock and didn't ever want to hear from me again."

"What did you do?"

"I sat down next to my things and cried. I was so hurt. I didn't understand. We had a couple of arguments but nothing I thought would make him that angry. I felt so disrespected. He didn't even have the courage to tell me to my face and allow me to pack up my clothes and leave with dignity. I didn't know where to go, so I called a friend from work. She said I could stay with her and her husband for a few nights. It was humiliating."

Mason got up from the couch and went to the kitchen to pour himself a fresh cup of coffee. Daniel watched him move languidly with a slight slump in his shoulders. He tried to imagine the mental anguish and turmoil brewing inside Mason and thought of how Mason was a model of opposites contained within the same vessel. He was the likes of which Daniel had never met nor gotten to know. On the exterior, Mason was smooth, projecting a self-confident and elegant face and demeanor. Always perfectly coifed and impeccably dressed. But not now. He watched as Mason poured his coffee and stirred in some half-and-half and artificial sweetener. When Mason picked up his cup and turned to return to the front room, Daniel quickly averted his gaze so Mason wouldn't think he was studying him.

Mason eased himself down onto the couch, but instead of curling up again, he sat up with both feet on the carpet. His face indicated consternation combined with thought, as if he was trying to figure out a puzzle. "Don't you find this all absurd?" he asked.

Daniel was surprised by the abruptness of the question and quickly tried to make sense of it but couldn't. "Absurd? How do you mean? Us? Right now?"

"No, life in general. I watched my family be so vested in the pursuit of money and status. Everything had to be perfect. But for what? After all those years making their lives perfect, they're now in bad shape. My mother is in an assisted-living facility, and my dad struggles to get around. He's too proud to go into a facility. I suspect arthritis, but he won't admit to anything being wrong. He says it's just old-age aches and pains. It's almost comical."

"Do you find their situation humorous?"

Mason shook his head. "Of course not, but in a sense it is hilarious." He frowned and took a sip of his coffee. "Don't you love irony? You know, you're the only one I can talk to. The only one I talk to."

"You have other friends, though, don't you? Your coworkers?"

Mason cast his eyes down and stared into his coffee. After a few minutes, he looked back up at Daniel. "I'm really tired. Would you be a dear and come back and check in later?"

"I'm not sure I can, but I'll try. I have other commitments later today and over the next couple of days." He stood up. "Honestly, I didn't think you'd be here. I just stopped by to water your plants and feed the fish like you asked me to."

"That's okay. I understand. I didn't think I would be either." He slid back down and lay on his side. "I love you, Daniel. I wish I could be better for you."

Daniel placed his hand on Mason's head. "I love you too. I'll get back to you as soon as I can."

18

THE EARLY EVENING, late summer sunlight filtered through leaves on the swaying tree branches outside his window and cast dappled shadows across Daniel's room. A gentle warmth that felt comforting filled the room. It was a welcome relief from the intense day, and he felt drained yet stirred.

Vincente had texted him to let him know that not only was Sophia in town, he was too, staying at their Cherry Creek condo, which served as their home base in Colorado. He and Vincente had agreed to get together, and he looked forward to Vincente dropping by with the hope his old friend would provide some solace and help him make sense of the chaos in his life. He decided on a snifter of Baileys to take the edge off the wait.

As he sipped, he allowed his mind to roam. Somehow the atmosphere in his room reflected his feelings, but then again, it didn't. He thought the word incongruity, but that didn't quite get at it. There was a better word for it, but that word was escaping him. He searched his mind and began to hum the tune of Paul Simon's "The Dangling Conversation," hearing the lyrics in his mind as he hummed. At last he came to it:

syncopated. He jotted it on his sketch pad and circled it. Out of tune. Offbeat. Not harmonious. He reached for his journal and began writing an entry about his visit with Sophia followed by the one with Mason. At the sounds of a tap on the door and Vincente's voice, he lifted his head and put his pen down.

"Good time to crash your party?" Vincente asked as he came in.

Daniel chuckled. "Some party. Hard to celebrate in the company of one."

"Well, now there's two of us." Vincente gently massaged Daniel's shoulder as he passed him. "Good to see you, my friend." He sniffed Daniel's drink. "Baileys?"

"Of course. It's on the cabinet. Pour yourself one."

"Maybe. Any tequila?"

"Always. It's in the cabinet, but it's not the top-shelf you prefer."

"I'll condescend and imbibe with the proletariat. I only ask that you keep this confidential."

"Your secret is safe."

After pouring his drink, Vincente settled into the chair across from Daniel's rocker and pointed to Daniel's pad and journal. "What are you writing about?"

Daniel held the pad up for Vincente to see.

"Syncopated," Vincente said. "Interesting. Broken, condensed, like a contraction. I don't get it."

Daniel set the pad on his lap. "Neither do I, but for some reason it seems to fit."

"Fit?"

"Me. My life. The chaos and turmoil in it. I suspect that on the surface, when someone looks at me, they probably conclude all is well. But you and I—and now Sophia—know all's not well. There's so much swirling. I can't get my head around one thing before another crops up. I feel like I'm against the ropes with Ali pummeling at will. It's coming at me too fast."

Vincente nodded. "Is that a bad thing?"

Daniel looked incredulously at Vincente. "A bad thing? Of course it is! Why do you ask that?"

"You tell me."

Daniel shook his head. "Please, old friend. Please don't use that psychologist's trick of turning a patient's question back to them."

"Well, my friend, it's not a trick or a strategy. It's a point to be taken. In such situations, most always, the answer lies within the person asking it. Vocalizing your query is your mind's way of expressing its inability or frustration to find an answer." He leaned forward and pointed toward Daniel's chest, raising his voice. "But it's in there. The answer is in there. And you know it. So don't try to bullshit me playing innocent and feigning you don't know it. You do know the answer, but you refuse to acknowledge it because in doing so, you would be admitting that you aren't some superman, some strong, fearless lion. It's high time you recognize you're just like everyone else—flawed and imperfect."

Daniel said nothing in reply. Vincente's salvo had come quickly, as if he'd come loaded for bear. It stunned him to the point of being unable to respond. Vincente's words seemed like an invective, but Daniel knew they weren't. They were harsh and pointed, but he knew they came from a place of love and caring.

Vincente went on, his voice softened but firm. "Daniel, you're strong. You act with courage. There isn't a perceived injustice you won't stand up to or a hurt soul you won't defend and care for. Except one: *you*. You cover up all your anxieties and struggles. You won't own up to your true desires and wishes, which have languished inside for sixty-odd years waiting to be acknowledged and honored. But you don't fool me. You never have. I saw through the veneer right off. I've never said that to you before, but I'm saying it now because it's time. In fact, past time. You know what I'm talking about. So let's no longer step around the horseshit and get to sloshing right through the muck."

Daniel sat rigidly, but his eyes misted as he smiled weakly.

Vincente glared at him. "Did I say something funny?"

Daniel shook his head. "No. Something you said reminded me of a story Jonathan told me from when he was a young man still living at home. He said his mother wanted him to go to his sister's farm and get her some manure. 'Don't get me that dried-up cow poop,' she told him. 'Bring me that fresh horse manure. That's what makes the garden grow best.'

"Jonathan would refer to it and laugh when he talked about his garden. He'd say, 'If I had fresh horseshit, my plants would be twice as full and luscious and my life would be all the better.'"

Vincente eased back into his chair. "So is there a metaphor in that?"

Daniel pursed his mouth and nodded. "I guess so. Thanks, Ali. I certainly wasn't expecting you to launch into me. It didn't feel good and still doesn't, but I guess I needed that." He took a sip of his Baileys, took a deep breath, and took one more sip. "Well, Ali, now that you've beaten me to a pulp, where to now?"

Vincente shrugged. "You tell me."

"Okay, I will. Or try to. Let's go back to what got us going: why everything coming so fast and overwhelming me might not be a bad thing. I can see it a bit more clearly now. I guess I needed to be or still need to be beaten down before I can get to the core of what's going on. You're right, Vincente, I've built a wall around myself. I suppose everyone puts up their own version of barricades, but I think that is especially true for gay men and even truer for those of us who operate and socialize primarily in the straight culture. And by straight, I mean homophobic, if not overtly, then subtly. That veneer, that shield is what helped get me through the crap and survive."

"Let me ask you this. Do you recall the *Merrimack* and *Monitor?*"

Daniel was surprised by the question. "Yes. They were the ironclads that battled in the Civil War."

Vincente nodded. "I'm not sure where they are now. I think one or both sank but might've been salvaged. But it's no matter. When I think of them, I think of the men inside them trapped and encased in iron. Each ironclad was able to launch fusillades against the other, and they were both impenetrable to their enemy's counterattack. But they fought on in a futile attempt to sink each other. It didn't work. I believe the battle was a draw. No one won."

Daniel sat quietly, processing the implications of Vincente's analogy. He sipped the last drops of his snifter, got up, and motioned to Vincente's glass. "Another?"

Vincente handed Daniel his glass. "Please."

After refreshing their drinks, Daniel picked up the thread of conversation. "Interesting metaphor. Like the Church and me. Two titans going at each other. But the hard truth is that neither of us will win because neither of us can be defeated. Like Moby Dick, I'm unconquerable, and the Church will be here long after I'm gone. But the question I still need to answer is this: Where to now? Do I need to answer that one for myself as well?"

"I'll throw you a lifeline. Ready to answer hard questions?"

"Now that you stripped me of my armor and I'm buck naked before you, why not?"

Vincente laughed. "We'll leave that image as a metaphor. The best way would be to peel the onion is a layer at a time rather than chopping and mincing it. Let's scan through pieces of your life. Don't dwell on the questions. Speak from the heart and just give a simple yes or no answer or at least only a few thoughts in response. Later, you and I or you and Sophia can delve more deeply into the wider aspects of them and flesh them out."

"Okay."

"You mentioned the Church within the context of the ironclads I spoke of. That suggests it's first and foremost—the most driving issue for you. Maybe it's not, but we can figure that out later. So when you think of the Church, is your thought generally favorable or unfavorable?"

"Mixed."

"Do you like where you are now in terms of your position?"

"Yes."

"Think of Jonathan. Do you love him?"

"Yes."

"Mason. Do you love him?"

Daniel hesitated before replying. "Yes, but."

"But what?"

"But not how I love Jonathan."

"Think of Rafael and Miguel. How do you see them?"

"Rafael is wounded in need of protection and rescuing."

"And Miguel?"

"I'm not sure." Daniel paused and stared at his drink for a moment. "But there's something else."

"What?"

"I'm not sure." He shrugged and shook his head. "I think I need to process it more before I can talk about it. I just know there's something else when it comes to Miguel."

"Okay," Vincente said. "Fair enough. I've saved the toughest for last. Ready?"

"Yes."

"Do you love Daniel Patrick Murphy?"

Daniel stared at Vincente, stunned by the question, and his mind swirled. He wanted to say that of course, he loved himself, but he couldn't.

Vincente leaned forward and placed his hand on Daniel's knee. "I'll save you a bit more here. Of course you love yourself, but by your nonanswer it seems there's at least one part of you that you don't love. All self-reflecting people know in their heart the things within them they don't like. But when the things inside we don't like become too strong, so powerful that they shape and even dictate our behavior, we begin to more than dislike them. The dislike morphs into contempt. In time, we come to loathe and be disgusted by them, and that becomes a problem because too often we conflate that loathing with our whole self. If not dealt with, it can go to the ultimate step—self-hatred. And those filled with self-loathing become destructive, either to themselves or to others. I truly don't believe that's where you are, but you will get to that place unless you take steps to intervene with yourself."

He eased back into his chair and sipped his tequila while Daniel sat quietly, reflecting. Neither spoke for several minutes.

Finally, Daniel spoke. "You're right, Vincente. I understand. The fog seems to be lifting. It's not a pleasant sight. But your points do help answer both questions: why and where to. And it's given me further insight into another."

"And that is?"

"Self-loathing. Now I understand something that has always escaped me. Self-loathing is the true gay plague. I think I'm now beginning to understand Miguel and why the thought of being in contact makes me anxious. Maybe I see much of me in him. Maybe he's that younger me."

19

THE DOOR TO Sophia's office was ajar, and she was sitting at her table writing. Daniel tapped, and she turned and smiled.

"Come in, Daniel. Your timing is perfect. I was just touching up a few notes for my presentation at the Jungian conclave in Boulder next week." She motioned toward a chair. "Please, have a seat."

"Thanks, Sophia, for seeing me on short notice," he said as he settled into the chair and made himself comfortable.

Sophia got up and moved over to the chair next to Daniel. "Of course, Daniel. We can't anticipate when matters like these come up, but it's crucial we act on them when they do."

Daniel nodded. "I don't know if Vincente told you anything about the conversation he and I had the other night. If he did, that's okay. I told him and I'm telling you that I'm fine with you sharing information about me. I trust you both to the depths of my soul."

"In the interest of transparency, I can tell you that Vincente did share with me the broad outline of your talk, but he thought it would be better if I heard the specifics from you directly."

"Fair enough." Daniel shifted his weight and took a deep breath. "First, Vincente punched through my armor. It turns out the armor wasn't steel but papier-mâché. Either that or Vincente packs quite a wallop. Either way, he broke through and tore the shield from my eyes, revealing the truth about me. It turns out that I'm not, after all, the king of the jungle but more of a tabby."

"Pause there for a moment and think about that. Do you really think you're some docile, domesticated feline that lies about and sleeps on the windowsill in the warmth of the sun?"

"I get your point. No."

"Good. Let's operate from this proposition: You're not some fearless, untamed lion, but neither are you a house cat. Our job is to help you figure out who and what you are, and then we can work on how you can go about honoring and becoming your true, authentic self."

Daniel smiled. "Of course. I like that."

"Good. Let's begin with who you are. Tell me who Daniel Murphy is."

"Well, Daniel is a sixty-two-year-old man of Irish descent. He's a Jesuit priest and teacher. He has a strong passion for learning. His primary focus when teaching is literature, but he also loves to delve into theology, philosophy, and psychology in the course of his teaching."

"Why does he do that?"

"Because those disciplines are intricately intertwined. Every story about a person, real or fictional, inherently involves complications about their belief system. Or at least it ought to."

"When he's teaching a story, novel, play, or whatever, what does Daniel tend to focus on as the key element?"

"Well, for him, setting and conflict are essential, but in the end, it's about the characters, the character of their character. Why they do what they do."

"Suppose you're a character in a story, which you are. How would you describe and develop him?"

"Hmm. That's an interesting assignment. Let's see. I'd describe him as a toxic stew of conflicting urges and wants, but he's prohibited from acting on them."

"You say prohibited. Are any of those urges or desires forbidden or prohibited by the law?"

Daniel shook his head. "No, of course not."

"Then what or who is prohibiting him from acting on them?"

Daniel reflected on that question for a few moments. "I think I understand what you're getting at. Me. I am. In the end, I'm prohibiting myself from acting on them."

"So no one and nothing else has forced you to make those decisions. Is that a fair conclusion?"

"Yes."

"Including your faith?"

"Yes."

"Okay. Take a few deep breaths."

Daniel did as she bade but was still holding the last breath when she said, "Now, let's talk about why you found it urgent to see me."

Daniel exhaled and replied, "In our talk, Vincente pushed me in several areas. The most challenging area was love. He asked a series of questions, and I could answer most with simple responses except for two: the ones about me and Miguel. I now can see that the reason for my hesitation about loving myself was because I was confusing aspects of my psyche with who I am. What I don't like about myself was making me dislike or even hate myself in a way. I get that. But I still can't put my finger on why I couldn't give an answer about Miguel other than that he reminds me somehow of my younger self. At least that's what I thought. And it might be true, but I'm now suspecting that it is or might involve something else I cannot identify. And I find that disturbing."

"Why?"

"Why do I find it disturbing?"

Sophia nodded.

"It's not because it's some nebulous unknown. I think it's because it might tell me something about myself I don't want to know. And it scares the hell out of me."

"Do you sense your fear might have something to do not only with Miguel reminding you of your young self—and perhaps some dark aspect from your past you have sequestered into your shadow—but also how you feel about him?"

Daniel was taken aback. "You mean that I might love him? Be in love with him? It can't be."

"Why not?"

"Well, he's a former student and nearly half my age."

"So?"

"So? I couldn't. It can't be."

"What if the answer to your second statement that it can't be is that it is. What then?"

Daniel shook his head violently. "That would be crazy! I couldn't! I can't!"

Sophia's voice became softer. "Daniel, it's not crazy and neither are you. You're a human being. A man. A gay one at that. Slow down and collect your thoughts. Let's go back to how you defined yourself earlier. I want to call your attention to a telling aspect of your being that you failed to include."

"That is?"

Sophia said nothing immediately, and Daniel reviewed in his mind what he'd said earlier. He shook his head and looked at Sophia inquisitively.

"Think of the ones in your life you hold most dear, those you might love intimately or be in love with."

"Ah, I see it now. I'm gay. I hadn't realized that I omitted that part of me."

"Take a moment and reflect on that omission. How do you feel knowing you failed to include that essential element of your being?"

"I feel embarrassed, even a bit ashamed. I guess it says something about me, something I keep denying even as I act on it." He thought about the profundity of his statement, his self-admission. "I say I act on it, but in truth, my acting on it is done only furtively, even with Jonathan. It's as if I've simply expanded the size of my closet." He looked at Sophia sheepishly.

She nodded. "Daniel, as a gay man, you have a natural affinity for men. Perhaps an attraction to a certain type of man—physically, intellectually, where interests are concerned. What attracts one person to another? The answers are unique to every person. A major inconsistency between straight and gay cultures is that on one hand, the same general rules of human attraction are at play. They're universal. But on the other hand, gays are not allowed to abide by their natural impulses.

"I'm sure you're aware of May-December marriages in which an older and a younger person, sometimes decades apart, come together, marry, and often live happy, fulfilled lives. While not the norm, we tend not to question why they become entwined, though that's more true if the older person is male. Still, in straight culture, even if the older person is female, while it might raise a few eyebrows and be fodder for gossip, society tends to accept them. But that doesn't seem to be the case for gay men. So the question for us to consider is why the May-December relationship for gay couples is taboo."

Daniel lifted his water bottle and sipped. "I understand your point, but when I think of Miguel, I'm not sure that's how I love him, if love for him is what I feel."

"Then what is it?"

"I don't know. I really don't. Something inscrutable. Something beautiful but terrifying."

"You say you haven't seen him since graduation. So there must be something from those days that has lingered and perhaps incubated since then."

Daniel closed his eyes and reflected, taking a deep breath and slowly exhaling it. After a few moments, he continued. "I have a confession to make. I have seen Miguel since high school. Once. It was a few years ago. I ran into him in a gay bar. I was stunned when he approached me."

"What did you do?"

"What *could* I do? I was outed. I broke into a cold sweat, but we talked. I bought him a drink. I had only one, which I nursed, so I felt okay to drive. But he was intoxicated. I drove him to his apartment. When we got there, he insisted I come up and see it. I sensed that I would be courting trouble if I did, but I went up anyway. I couldn't seem to resist. After we went in, he said he had to use the bathroom. When he came back out, he was wearing only a pair of black leather shorts. I was stunned again. I got up and started to leave, but he said he wasn't trying to lure me, that it was the way he always dressed at home."

"Did you leave?"

"No, but it was okay. I sat on a side chair and he curled up on his couch. And we just talked: philosophy, psychology, even literature. He mentioned a number of the novels I'd had my classes read that impacted him."

"So you didn't touch him?"

"No, other than a hug when I left a couple of hours later."

"Did you want to?"

"He had a magnificent body, but no, I didn't want to. Plus, there was something else."

"What?"

"It would've defiled something of sublime beauty. There was something about Miguel, something wild and uncontrollable but somehow disciplined. He had kind of a princely, regal mien. Thinking back on it and on him, maybe that's what drew me to him. To this day, I cannot put my finger on why, but somehow my life shifted at that moment in time."

"Do you suspect that uncontrollable wildness is what you've suppressed, repressed, and locked away in your shadow?"

Daniel nodded. "It might be. Maybe that's my ultimate fear. When I was leaving, he wrote his number on a slip of paper and gave it to me. He said he would never tell anyone about our meeting and that he would not call me. It would be up to me to call him. I knew our secret was safe. It's strange. Aside from Jonathan, Vincente, and you, the only other person I trust completely to the bottom of my soul is Miguel. He might have all kinds of problems, but when he gives his word, he keeps it."

"Have you called him?"

Daniel shook his head.

"Have you been tempted to?"

He nodded.

"Will you call him now?"

Again he nodded. "But there's one thing I need to do before I call him."

"What's that?"

"Something I've been stewing over for a long time."

20

"HOW'S THE MARGARITA, Daniel?" Vincente asked.

"Perfect as always."

"*Bueno.*"

"And thanks again. I hesitated before texting to see if it would be okay for me to come back down, thinking you might want a bit of down time after you got back. But I really needed to talk."

"Say no more. Let me take care of a few things in the kitchen. In the meantime, soak in that sweet, aromatic smell of sage and gaze at the sky. Their healing powers are miraculous."

"Thank you, my old friend."

Daniel sunk lower into the chaise lounge, tilted his head back, and breathed in slowly. The sweet smell of the damp sage of the New Mexican high desert blessed his lungs. He inhaled deeply, held the breaths, and slowly exhaled. It had an intoxicating, balmy effect. More than that of the margarita. Or maybe it was a wondrous mix of the two. It didn't matter. He couldn't get enough. He smiled to himself as he wondered if overdosing on the smell of sage was possible. If so, it wasn't a bad way to go.

He stared up into space and wondered if there were other sentient life beings out there. If there were, did they ever feel as depleted as him? He took a sip and held the sweetness of the margarita on his tongue. The taste, the sensation, the pleasure. Pleasure. He ruminated on the concept and toyed with it in his mind. Simple pleasure. Bountiful pleasures. Restricted and most of them taboos in the priesthood. He couldn't recall who said that a life filled with pleasure was dissolute. Probably some ancient Greek stoic or Church father. But, he mused, he wasn't thinking of a life filled with pleasure, just one with some pleasure. Even sinful on occasion. Now he could be hedonistic if he wanted to be. He smiled lasciviously, but as quickly as he smiled, the ache in his chest returned. He closed his eyes and slowly breathed into it, holding the breath for an eight-count and exhaling it more slowly than he'd inhaled. It helped, but the ache remained, as did the longing.

The sound of Vincente moving and settling into his chair jarred him. Vincente reached over and tapped Daniel's hand. "Thank you for coming, my friend."

"You and Sophia have been most accommodating. I hit her up on short notice yesterday, and she, too, didn't hesitate. Maybe we should've carpooled," he jested.

Vincente chuckled. "I guess we could've, but maybe it was better for us not to. It certainly gave you some alone time. But always keep in mind that there's no such thing as short notice for you, Daniel, and you're welcome to stay as long as you like. And if neither of us is here, you have the run of the place.

You've been through the mill, and it's going to take time for you to regain your strength. Rest, sleep, read, meditate, or go for a walk or drive." He noticed Daniel's empty glass. "Can I pour you another?"

Daniel handed his glass to Vincente. "*Por favor.*"

"Sophia gave me just an overview of what you and she talked about," Vincente said as he lifted the decanter. "She said it would be best for you to share the details when you're ready."

"Yes, you two are quite good at that." Vincente raised an inquisitive eyebrow as he handed Daniel his drink. "I'm only kidding. It's my feeble attempt at wry humor. I understand why you both leave it to me to offer the details."

"No need to explain." He paused before going on. "Daniel, you talk when it works for you. But it's important to talk about it before too long. Otherwise, it can settle back into your subconscious, and when we do that, we tend to keep it locked again. Then it can harden and fester. Right now you're pliable, vulnerable. Your natural instinct is to toughen up and put it away. But you have to resist doing that. Once the spigot is open, it's crucial for it to remain open until all the toxicity is expelled. So, my friend, my brother, let it out."

Daniel nodded. "I know you're right. It's why I came here. I knew you wouldn't allow me to stow it away. And you're the only one I can speak completely freely to. Even though I can now speak freely with Sophia, there's still a line between us—a professional one. That's important. There are times when our problems need to be handled clinically. But at other times, like now, I don't need a shrink. I need a drink and a friend. And I have the best one in the world."

Vincente reached over, grabbed Daniel's hand, and firmly squeezed it. After a moment, he released it and sat back in his chair. He said nothing, apparently waiting for Daniel to continue.

Daniel took a deep breath and began. "I sent my letter to all the proper authorities asking to be given dispensation from my vows and to become laicized. It was the hardest thing I've ever done, as I'm sure you understand. As you know, I've mulled it over and over, but I was always resistant to act on it. In hindsight, I can understand why. For me, there's no going back, no putting the genie back in the bottle. Once done, it's done."

Vincente nodded in assent.

"So you have to be sure. I recall you saying that you had clarity when it came to making the call. You knew what you wanted and didn't want. Me, I have no clarity. I'm in a fog, feeling my way through the mist. But while I have no clarity, I have the sense that this is what I need to do."

Daniel turned to Vincente and shrugged. "In other words, I understand why I need to leave the priesthood, but I'm at a loss about what to do or where to go next."

"Well, my friend, you taught about the *where to* for many years. It's called the journey, and a journey doesn't just happen at the beginning of one's young adulthood and end at some mystical point. Everyone's journey is a lifelong experience. And within the overall journey are multiple legs of it. We often generalize or categorize them and call them life stages—youth, young adulthood, middle age, and so on—but from that perspective, a life journey becomes linear, a birth-to-death experience. It flattens one's life. When you're a kid, you do this or that. When you're an adult, you find a career and maybe start a family. And when you become old, you're to be a grandparent, play golf, or whine about the travails of old age." He shook his head. "It's so St. Paul.

"For some, a select few in my professional opinion, the life journey is full of twists and turns that, like yours, never end up in serene retirement. They go on and on, ceaselessly searching until they drop. The worst hell on earth for them would be living out their later years in an assisted-living facility or lying in a health care facility on a ventilator with feeding tubes stuck in them helping them prolong life artificially.

"Daniel, all journeys, even the legs of a journey, have launch points. You've crossed a threshold. But first things first. Before you go on and ruminate about what the future portends, it's crucial to review what led up to and ultimately caused you to want to cross this threshold at this stage in your life because one thing you never want to do is look into your life's rearview mirror and have regrets."

"It's interesting. An image of me at the threshold came to mind when you mentioned one. Before crossing it, I turned around. And the scene wasn't in fog. It was sharp and crystal clear. And now that I'm thinking of it, I recall that image arising in my dreams."

"What did you see?"

"The Basilica of St. Peter in Rome and lying in St. Peter's Square curled up in a fetus position. Jonathan was down on one knee behind me massaging my neck."

"Whoa! That's a powerful image. Talk about it."

"Obviously, the basilica was symbolic of the Church. I recall that when you asked my feelings about it, I said they were mixed. They still are. When I think of James, Richard, and the thousands of priests—and even a few bishops—who do the right thing and actually nurture their flocks by speaking about and modeling love and compassion, I see richness and beauty, the message Jesus spoke about in the first part of the Sermon on the Mount. When I witness lay Catholics who actually practice true Christian values, such as volunteering and administering to the poor and hungry, I'm humbled. They help me renew my belief in the resurrection. But then there's the institution itself, and at times I become apoplectic."

Daniel realized he was agitated and got up from the chaise to pace. "And there I was, a grown, older, sophisticated, intelligent man curled in a fetal position, trembling. The symbolism is unsettling. I think of it as lying outside the womb of Mother Church. I also see it as debasing, like I've been reduced to a child, an infant cowering before some majesty. And it was Jonathan, the Buddhist, comforting me, not judging but consoling and conveying compassion—something I cannot recall ever getting from the Church." He glared down at Vincente, and his next words were forceful. "The greatest irony about the Church is that she talks about forgiveness and compassion, but she only forgives and offers compassion on her terms."

"Like Kali," Vincente interjected.

Daniel looked at him inquisitively and sat back down on the chaise.

"Kali," Vincente explained, "is a Hindu mother goddess. She's stern and can be a wrathful mother. It seems that is how you're now seeing the Catholic Church. Not so much as a tender mother as pictured by the Madonna but as an unforgiving, judgmental one."

Daniel slowly nodded several times, but he still felt agitated.

Vincente swung his legs around, stood, and reached down for Daniel's hand. "Daniel, it's imperative that you talk about this and get it out, once and for all. But take a break so you can talk about it more dispassionately. Use the facilities and splash some cool water on your face and neck. And do some stretching. It will help ease the compaction you're feeling."

Daniel assented, grasped Vincente's wrist, and allowed Vincente to pull him up. In the bathroom, he splashed cool water over his head, allowing the coolness to sink into and envelop his hair and skull. It felt refreshing. As he toweled off, he stared at the visage in the mirror. It was haggard, and the face was drawn and lean. He stretched his jaw and noticed that when he closed his mouth, his molars no longer touched. He began massaging his jaw and felt a previously undiscovered tenderness, but when he worked his jaw back and forth, trying to relax, he could feel the tension easing.

When he raised his arms and forced his shoulders back, he felt the tightness in his upper back and massaged it by squeezing his shoulder blades as tight as he could, then leaning slightly forward and scrunching his shoulders together in front of him. He repeated the exercise several times, imagining an accordion. Then he bent forward to touch his toes. He could not. So he just hung forward, allowing his arms to hang loosely to pull his weight downward. After a few moments, he slowly raised himself and could feel his blood flowing. A mixture of warmth and coolness pervaded his body, so he repeated the exercise a few more times.

Feeling reinvigorated, he strode back out to the patio where Vincente was stretched out on his chaise lounge. Daniel noticed a fresh decanter of margarita mix and plate of nachos. Vincente pointed to the platter of cheese-covered nachos that sat near Daniel's side of the table.

"Better dig in before the cheese cools," he said. "It's always best when the cheese is warm and gooey."

"Thanks, Vincente. I feel much, much better."

"Good. You look better. Even in the dim light, I can see some color back in your face. Ready to go on?"

"I am, but only after I kill off these nachos and chase them with a fresh margarita. It seems I've worked up an appetite." He chewed slowly and then coughed. "Oof! Those are some hot chili peppers."

Vincente waved a hand at him. "It's that soft Irish blood flowing through you."

Daniel gave his friend a stink eye. "One thing the Irish are not is soft." After a moment, they both guffawed and then grew silent.

Daniel wiped his hands on the paper napkin as he chewed on the last morsel and set the plate and napkin on the table. "You know, Vincente, it's dawning on me how jealous I am of Jonathan. He's a complex man and he's a thinker, yet he's been able to reduce life to relative simplicity. It's not a simplicity of faith as much as one of acceptance. I've never been able to do that. I keep thinking that there must be something more, something beyond our knowing. He thinks that too, but he's comfortable with not knowing. He still wonders and ponders about what he calls the God Unknown, but I keep searching for the God Known. I'm not as comfortable with ambiguity as he is. I want certainty. Or at least I thought I wanted certainty. But now that I'm in this fog of uncertainty, I don't know how to react. He'd say, just be and savor the time in the unknown."

He paused to think a moment. "Maybe that's the fundamental difference between him and me. He relishes going off-trail, literally and figuratively. I need to stick to paths and roads already hewed and paved. And for me, one of them has been the Church."

"Why do you suppose you think and feel that way?"

"I don't know. Perhaps it's because it's a natural, intrinsic part of my nature. Although I never aspired to be the top dog in any group or organization I've been part of, I have a take-charge type of personality. I'm a Leo by birth, so it may be related to my sun sign, but that's really almost irrelevant. If one is a leader, he better know what the purpose of the mission is and where the hell he's going. Leading a life of uncertainty or ambiguity doesn't bode well for leader types like me.

"But I also understand that the other side of leading is following, and sometimes leaders need to follow. But what if someone is a leader type like me and he's been resolutely following his own leader only to finally see that leader as both fallible and errant? What if he's had unshakable faith in that leader but now loses faith and confidence in him? Then what? He finds himself leaderless and sets off into an area in which he has no experience or expertise. His natural instinct is to lead, but all those inclinations and skills fail him, and he has no one to follow."

"Ah, yes," Vincente replied. "It's called being a trailblazer. It's a rare but critical archetype. But before you go too far into that, talk about why you lost faith in the Church. It's one thing to let all the factors ruminate in your mind but quite another to verbally express them. When we search for the right words to express why we believe or feel as we do, it helps focus the mind. So give voice to your reasons for leaving the priesthood and the Jesuits in particular."

"First, let me make clear it isn't my faith I've lost, but my faith in the Church. That said, as I said earlier, I recognize and honor the good so many Catholics, lay and clerics, do.

But lately, what the institution has done that has caused great harm and peril to so many others, Catholics and non-Catholics alike, has become untenable in my conscience. Even unforgiveable. It has begun to outweigh the good.

"I keep qualifying my statement by pointing to the good people within religious institutions who don't hold to diabolical precepts, but in truth, the seed of much hatred and dehumanization lies under the broad umbrella of religion in the form of the Church. And that holds whether it's hostility toward sexual orientation, hostility toward people who have divorced, or animosity toward other religious persuasions. Moral judgment and condemnation of the world beyond its scope are part and parcel of monotheism. And that notion has had deplorable consequences for so many people over the past millennia. I wonder how many have been persecuted and died in the name of religion."

Daniel turned toward Vincente and shook his head. "Vincente, I can no longer be part and parcel to such a belief system. And yet … and yet, I still believe. I just don't know what, and unlike my dear Jonathan, I need to know."

"I see," Vincente replied.

"But this is about something far greater than the Church," Daniel said. "This is about me, my soul. Up to now, I've lived my life in large part for others and structured it to be in accordance with the extraneous rules laid down by them. But now I've come to understand that many of them—the ideas and some of the people—are harmful to my being and destructive to my being my true self—becoming individuated, as Carl Jung termed it, and living fully as I believe I was created to live. I can go on and blame, but in the end, I made the decisions to live as I did. I accept that and blame no one and nothing else."

"So why did you become a priest?"

"Good question. I ponder that to this day, not out of regret, because I have none, but as something to reflect on and learn from. Ironically, I never saw serving in the priesthood as a calling. I never felt God called me. It was something I chose to do, and it was something I became damn good at as a profession. That might seem incongruent, but that's my truth. My best answer is that something drew me to it. There was something mysterious and profound about what a priest does in the act of transubstantiation.

"One time when I was at Jonathan's, I was reading one of Joseph Campbell's essays. In it he spoke about the *mysterium tremendum*—a tremendous, awe-inspiring, yet terrifying mystery. I was struck by that. When I brought it up to Jonathan in a discussion, he took a different point of view on it. In his mind, as humans, we aren't witnesses to that *mysterium tremendum,* we're part of it. I still can't get my head around that notion. And that, my dear friend, is one of the angels I am spiritually grappling with. Am I part of the Creative Force, or am I outside of it, a by-product of the Creator?"

"So are you imprisoned in the lions' den wrestling with a lion," Vincente interjected, "or are you the lion clawing and tearing at the portal, determined to break out?"

Daniel reflected quietly on Vincente's philosophical query as he tilted his head back and stared at the stars. The plentitude of them relative to what he was used to in a more populated setting struck him anew. Vincente's question clarified his quandary. It was more than a question of who he was. It was also a question of where he was and where he fit in the whole.

"That's the question," Daniel finally said. "I'm determined to be the fundamental, essential me, but finding out who he is scares the living shit out of me."

"Good. You're facing what lies ahead with true courage. So where to next?"

"I'll be heading back to Denver in a day or two. Before I go, I do want to go back and check out that spiral staircase at the Loretto Chapel more closely. I'd love for you to go with me if you're of a mind to and have the time."

Vincente gave him a thumbs-up.

"Vincente, my friend, there's something more." Vincente raised his eyebrows. "On a hunch, or maybe it was precognition, I applied for a sabbatical last spring. It's been approved, and it begins shortly, at the beginning of the fall semester. Hopefully, by the time the next semester rolls around in January, I will be defrocked and may be a persona non grata by the Church. In any event, I will be leaving the vicarage soon."

Daniel could feel emotion washing over him and paused to wipe his eyes with the sleeves of his shirt before continuing. Vincente said nothing, but the look on his face spoke of the caring that had evolved during their long friendship. Daniel knew Vincente appreciated that this was almost as big a step for him as leaving the priesthood.

"Jonathan has agreed to meet in Chaco Canyon the first of next week," he finally said. "I'll share the news with him there. I'm excited to get there. I went with him once many years ago but only saw it as a historical site of ruins from ancient indigenous people. But now, I think I'm beginning to sense what Jonathan feels about the place, which is that there's something profound and sacred about it. From there? To be determined."

Daniel swung his legs around and pushed himself up from the chair. Vincente also got up, and the two began gathering the plates and glasses. As they ambled toward the kitchen, Daniel gazed up at the night sky and paused.

"And there is the one I've been reluctant to talk to." He looked at Vincente as he walked through the door. "After I left Sophia's office, I remembered Stephen asked me to give him a heads-up about what I decided. I texted him and said I'll reach out to Miguel. We'll see how that goes."

Vincente patted Daniel's shoulder as he stepped by. "It will be interesting, to say the least. By the way, I'll be heading up that way myself to meet Sophia. We're flying out of DIA next week for Spain. I have some family history I want to dig into. So I'll pop over to have a bite with you, James, and Richard if Maggie will have me."

"Have you? She'll bake up her best Mexican cuisine in your honor. But let me know the day you plan to come. It might well be my last supper there."

"No Irish stew in honor of your last supper?"

"Hmm. Good question. Let's see who ranks higher in her esteem. I bet it's you."

21

FATHER DANIEL PATRICK Murphy surveyed the scene from the doorway into his room. For once, his room was orderly. His desk, infamous for chaotic heaps of student papers, unread memos, and lesson plans, was clear. His bed was made, the corners tucked, and the pillow plumped. Late summer dappled rays warmed the room. He took in the familiar sight of his books lining the shelves, once haphazardly but now in stately order. Taking a deep breath, he entered and went to the bathroom to wash up. He'd lost weight. A lot of it. He'd punched extra holes in his belt and his shirt hung on him. He felt drained, yet not weak. Changed. Changing.

When he stepped back into the bedroom, he went over to his old rocker and rocked it gently, smiling at the soft squeaks. He scanned his old friends on the shelves, novels and a menagerie of other works, tattered, worn, and dog-eared. How much they had meant to him. They had helped him through the crises of his life, and he'd taught their lessons to both eager and not so eager minds. The thought of leaving them was unpleasant, but leave them he must. Maggie would pack them for storage until a time when he could return and retrieve them like lost orphans or when their purpose and owner had been forgotten and they found their way to a thrift store or recycle bin.

His bags, bulged with trousers, shirts, socks, underclothes, and personal toiletries, sat waiting at the foot of his bed. Give all ye have to the poor, he thought, and ye shall have treasure in heaven. He didn't have much to give other than books, but that was fitting.

A rap accompanied by Maggie's voice came through the door. "Father, Brother Vincente has arrived. He's with Father James and Father Richard in the study."

Daniel opened the door to the woman who had been like a mother to him, despite the fact that they were close in age. "Thank you, Maggie. Remember, Vincente is no longer in the order and is happily married."

"Of course," she said mirthfully, "but he'll always be *Brother* Vincente in my heart."

Daniel took Maggie's hand as she stepped into the room and pulled her close. "How long have you been our mother, Maggie?"

"Mother. I do like that. I'm so blessed. All my sons are priests! Now, how many other old Irish women could say that?"

"I like it too. You were here when I came years ago."

"Aye. Near forty-four now for me. Every one of those years a blessed one. Except for when that cantankerous Father Higgins was here. He was a grumpy old soul."

"Thank you, Maggie." He leaned down and kissed her on her head. "What's for dinner on my last day?"

"Why, Irish stew, of course."

"Scones for dessert?"

"I couldn't forget my Scottish granny, now, could I? Now, you go down and visit with your friends. I have a small task to tend to before I set out dinner."

Daniel pulled the strap of the smaller bag over his shoulder, lifted the other, and took a last glance around the room. He smiled and nodded to Maggie as he turned to leave.

"Bless you, Father," Maggie said as she wiped a tear with her apron. "This room will be lonely without you."

James, Richard, and Vincente stopped their banter and stood when they saw Daniel. Each embraced him warmly, extending their affection with gentle comments.

James gestured to the overstuffed recliner on which he customarily sat. "Sit here. We're here to honor you."

"Allow me to pour the wine," Richard said as he lifted a decanter. "It's from my cousin's Upstate New York farm. Special edition, you know."

"I wasn't aware your family had a vineyard," Daniel replied.

"It runs in the family. Miceli. *Italiano.* My great-grandfather started it with shoots he smuggled from Tuscany."

Daniel sniffed the wine and sipped. "I'm not a connoisseur of wine, but this is wonderful."

"What about Irish whiskey?" Richard joshed. "Are you an expert there?"

"Of course. Along with dark malt beer."

"This is an evening for celebration, so it's good to go to our meal on a note of frivolity," James said. "But it's also a time of sadness. To both, let's toast our brother."

They raised their glasses toward each other.

"Have you heard the news of our old friend Archbishop Kelly?" James asked Daniel.

"I haven't."

"Well, it seems the Holy Father has a need for his services at the Vatican."

"I heard he had a nervous breakdown," Vincente said. "But that could just be rumor."

"I'm not so sure," James replied. "He hasn't been the most popular leader, considering his strict emphasis on tradition. The chancery is keeping an airtight seal on communiques. Regardless, I wish him a safe journey to Rome."

"More wine?" Richard asked, breaking a few moments of silence. After refreshing their glasses, Richard turned to Daniel. "Daniel, we will feel your absence profoundly. There's no question of that. But to be honest—and this is a time for honesty—James and I are wondering if you might be acting rashly in your decision to leave the priesthood."

Daniel sat quietly, alternating between staring at Richard and his glass. "Thank you, Richard, for being straightforward. And thank you, both of you, for your unfaltering support. I didn't come to this decision easily. I've been struggling with this for years—Jacob wrestling with the angel. I've had a growing dissatisfaction with where I am in life, and I've been even more dissatisfied with myself for resisting instead of pursuing what my soul yearns for. I've done my best to fulfill my obligations as both a priest and teacher, and there has been joy in doing so. But I've also deferred and even denied other joys."

He paused and looked at each of his friends' faces in turn. "Perhaps because I feared opprobrium and judgment from those whose opinions and respect I value, I've been living a lie. I'm in my early sixties and know the grains of sand in my hourglass of life are a precious few and declining in quality. I don't want to be looking down on my toes as I lie on my deathbed, ruing the fact that I spent my life inauthentically, neither living my truth nor pursuing happiness for myself. So while leaving the priesthood does come with a certain amount of loss, including the loss of a cherished brotherhood, it also comes with a chance for a new beginning, just in time before I become too old for new beginnings. And I'm choosing that new beginning."

"Daniel," James said, "no teacher, no priest has done more for his students or the community than you. While I'm saddened by your imminent departure, my heart is full of joy for you. My sadness is a selfish feeling, but my joy is genuine. Can I assume you mean to publicly affirm your relationship with Jonathan?"

Daniel raised an eyebrow. "No. Jonathan and I have already had that conversation. We are, as they say, no longer an item."

"I'm sorry to hear that," James said. "Hopefully, all is well between you and you'll remain within each other's heart."

"It is good between us. Though we will no longer be joined at the hip, I have much to learn from Jonathan." He paused and laughed. "And knowing him as I do, I have no doubt he'll be a great teacher. A stern one, in fact. I think he's become more in tune with the Zen discipline of Buddhism than the Tibetan tradition."

They all laughed.

"I'm heading to Chaco Canyon tomorrow. Jonathan agreed to meet me there. It's his spiritual center. We still have a lot to talk about, including my decision to leave the priesthood, and I couldn't think of a better place to have that conversation. It's been many years since I went there with him, and I'm in a completely different mindset than I was then. I want to see the place through my new lens. There's so much I want to learn of the place."

"Where are you staying tonight?" James asked.

"I reserved a room at a hotel near the Denver Tech Center, and I have one other friend to see this evening before heading out."

Vincente gave a small approving nod in acknowledgement of who that person was.

"You'll keep us posted?" Richard asked.

"Of course, my brothers. We're family, no matter the physical distance between us."

"Let's go to the dining room," James said as he stood. "I suspect Maggie has cooked up a special meal for your last day here."

Vincente inhaled a loud, exaggerated sniff. "Hmm, yes, it does smell like Irish stew." He punched Daniel in the arm as they walked out. "It looks like she favored you over me."

Daniel stopped, his mouth agape, as they entered the dining room. The room was festooned in Irish green: The table was covered with a green and white striped tablecloth, and above the table, from one corner to the other, hung crepe paper stringers with paper shamrocks dangling from them.

"Oh, my God," he said as his eyes misted.

"Maggie's idea," Richard admitted. "We helped cut the shamrocks under Maggie's watchful tutelage."

James pointed to the seat at the head of the table. "You sit there, Daniel, in the place of honor."

After they sat, Maggie handed Daniel a bundle wrapped in white tissue paper with a green ribbon and a bow.

"What's this?" he asked.

"Well, love," Maggie replied, "open it and find out."

Daniel slowly untied the green ribbon and pulled the paper apart. His eyes widened. "A quilt!" He unfurled it and stood so the others could see it. "It's made of my old running shirts." He turned to Maggie. "It's beautiful. I was wondering where they disappeared to."

Maggie put on her best innocent face. "One night, a little leprechaun appeared at the foot of my bed and said he found this pot of gold. When I looked in it, there they were."

Daniel pulled Maggie into a tight embrace. "It's the greatest and most beautiful gift I ever received. I will treasure it above all else to the end of my days. Thank you."

He turned to his friends. "And thank you for all."

Vincente reached under his chair and pulled up a small jug of Baileys. "And the leprechaun dropped this as he scurried out the door," he said conspiratorially." He poured them each a shot and stood, as did the others. "To our brother in arms."

"To our brother," James and Richard said as they lifted their glasses.

Daniel stood, dumbstruck, knowing he was experiencing the best moment of his life.

The conversation and celebration he had with his friends and the anticipation of meeting Miguel vied in his mind for dominance as he coursed along the Sixth Avenue Freeway toward Denver. When he pulled up to the stoplight at Broadway, his eyes lit up at the sight of the city lights. Though he was not a big city boy, Denver seemed to be just the right size for his comfort. It offered many cultural opportunities and charming venues to hang out in without so much that it was overwhelming.

Despite its growing population and increasing importance as a financial and economic center, Denver had not lost its cow town flavor for him. The city avoided the pretentiousness of other Old West towns that had boomed into major national and international centers of commerce, but he could still get lost in the masses.

He no longer felt the anxiety he experienced when he first began going to gay bars. Still, it would be his first time at the Lions' Den, which was in a part of Denver he wasn't familiar with. He felt a rising sense of anxiety as he made his way north on Lincoln Avenue and wondered if it was due to rendezvousing with Miguel or if it was because they were meeting at an unfamiliar bar that was, from what he understood, geared to the younger crowd. Both, he thought. But he hoped it would be fine.

As he suspected, the parking lot was full, but as he was about to pull back out onto the street, he saw a vehicle just ahead backing out. He stopped and flipped on his turn signal to indicate he was snagging that space. It was a tight squeeze, but at least he could park near the joint and not have to find street parking. He gingerly opened his door, quickly realized he had more space than he'd thought between his vehicle and the other, and wondered if it was another telling sign of aging.

A queue had formed at the entrance as the bouncer checked each ID closely, shining his light first on the guy and then on the card. After confirming that the ID was valid and the young man was of age, he'd simply toss his head in the direction of the door. Daniel watched him methodically scrutinize each incoming patron. Every so often, he did a double take at the man to be absolutely sure he was the real owner of the ID. It dawned on Daniel that it was primarily due to the changing hair styles and colors and facial accoutrements and adornments.

"Yeah, dude, that's me," he heard more than once over the top of the pulsing, throbbing music emanating from the interior.

He was relieved to see a few gray-haired men in line, though he knew he didn't fit their profile of beefy forty-somethings vainly attempting to hang on to their youth. He thought of how prevalent the Peter Pan archetype was throughout gay culture.

Puer aeturnus, the eternal boy. He felt just a little sorry for them because he understood, all too well, that age catches up with everyone if you stick around long enough.

After the bouncer gave the nod to the young men in front of him, Daniel started to hand over his driver license, but the bouncer just nodded toward the entry saying, "Enjoy your evening, sir."

Daniel smiled, winked, and mischievously replied, "Thank you, *sir,*" and strode in.

The place was packed, loud, and heavy with male sweat. Daniel turned sideways to push himself through the partying crowd. The dance floor across from the oval bar was filled with writhing bodies, mostly male but also a few females and several gender-neutral young people. The energy was high, and boisterous laughter and shouts added to the din. Daniel surveyed the bar but didn't see Miguel. He elbowed his way farther to the back of the room and finally spotted Miguel with Stephen sitting on barstools. Miguel was dressed in black. Combined with his black hair, the black attire added to the luster of his rich, olive skin, and he looked fit, angular, and serious. A Latino Adonis.

A moment later, Miguel glanced up and waved to him. A hint of a smile crossed his lips, and he stood as Daniel pushed the rest of his way through the crowd. They embraced.

"Good to see you, Miguel," Daniel shouted.

"Same. Thanks for coming." He kept an arm around Daniel's waist as he turned to his friend. "This is my old teacher, Daniel Murphy. And this is my friend, Stephen."

Daniel nodded and shook Stephen's hand. "We've met. Good to see you again, Stephen."

Miguel appeared to be a bit surprised as he pulled a third stool from the table and Daniel climbed aboard.

"Can I get you a drink?" Miguel asked.

"Thanks. Maybe a soda."

Miguel motioned to the waiter. "A Coke for my friend."

Daniel looked around the room, taking in the bright sights and the boisterous young people who were obviously having a great time. He smiled broadly and turned back toward Miguel. "Could you have picked a quieter place?"

Miguel grinned. "Next time."

Daniel turned toward Stephen, who appeared to be a bit uncomfortable and distracted. "Are you from here, Stephen?"

"No, sir. Tennessee. I go to the University of Denver. I transferred there during my junior year after I moved here."

"What are you studying?"

"Classical art and computer science. I can't make up my mind about which to major in. So maybe both."

"That's an interesting combination."

"It has its challenges, but then, I'm up for challenges." He gave a head nod toward Miguel.

"How did you meet Miguel?"

"I had a side gig dancing at Boyztown to make a few extra bucks and spotted Miguel at a table. After my set, I went over to him and acted all flirty, and he just stared at me. I was beginning to feel like an idiot, but when I turned to leave, he told me to stay and said he liked how I danced. At first I felt uncomfortable, but I've come to realize that even though he doesn't say much, when he does talk, he says much in few words."

Miguel reached over and squeezed Stephen's hand and then turned to Daniel. "I know this isn't the best place and time to catch up, so I'm wondering if we could get back together in the next few days."

"I'd love to but I'm leaving in the morning for a couple of weeks of much needed R and R. Doing a road trip south and then west. But I wanted to connect with you before pulling out."

"Are you heading all the way out to the coast?"

"I think so. I'm leaving for New Mexico in the morning to meet a friend. Then I'll head to Arizona to check out the Painted Desert and Petrified Forest. I remember going there with my parents when I was a boy. But eventually, I think I'll make it to the coast. If I do, I hope to drive up Highway One along the Pacific Coast. But I'll see."

"I wish I were going with you. I could use some time away from here myself. Care for some company?"

Daniel looked at him with surprise. "You mean go along with me?"

"Not at first. I have some personal time coming to me from my gig here at the bar. I'll see if I can take it now. If so, I could fly out to LA or some other place along your way." He paused and met Daniel's eyes. "No pressure."

Daniel took a sip of his soda. "Ah, sure. It might be fun to drive the highway with someone."

"Cool. I'll text you in a couple of days, and we can make final arrangements."

Daniel looked at his watch and started to get up. "I need to get going. I want to be on the road by six tomorrow morning."

Miguel stood and pulled Daniel into another embrace. "Thanks for coming by, old friend. We have lots to talk about, so maybe see you in Cali."

Daniel smiled. "Looking forward to it." He waved to Stephen. "I hope to see you again."

Outside the bar, Daniel sat in his vehicle and stared at the buildings across the street from the Lions' Den, his mind racing as he wondered what had just transpired. Of all the scenarios he could've concocted in his mind in anticipation of how meeting up with Miguel would turn out, a road trip with him would not have been part of any of them. He felt a cold sweat begin to rise, countered by a warm sense of excitement, as he fired up his truck's engine. As he made a left onto Walnut Street and slowly drove westward toward Broadway, he considered heading to the gay pub he had always gone to in the past to reflect on the insanity he'd just experienced. But he thought better of it and continued south toward the hotel where he had reserved a room.

"My life," he said aloud, "has become one crazy shitstorm. But all I can do is hang on until the Fates and Furies tire of wreaking their havoc."

He made a left from Broadway onto the ramp to take I-25 south. "It'll be good. Right? It'll be good."

22

THE AFTERNOON SUN stood high above the horizon as Daniel skated over the washboard dirt road in the New Mexico high desert. The tire thumps added to the rhythmic pulses of the Native American flutes and chants emanating from his sound system. Microscopic particles filtered the sun's bright light. Ahead, a moving yellow dust cloud created by another vehicle led the way, and a discernible taste of the dust found its way inside his vehicle. He would soon be meeting Jonathan at the Chaco Canyon Visitor Center, and thoughts raced through his mind about what to say and how to say it. He tried to dismiss them and kept telling himself that their next conversation would come about like every previous one had: unfolding as it was meant to. But he remained unconvinced.

There it is, he thought as the outline of Fajada Butte appeared on the horizon. Seeing no other vehicle in the rear-view mirror, he slowed to ingest the full power of the sight. He was struck by its presence and power and how it jutted up and dominated the valley, and he thought about how the indigenous peoples who flourished in the vast area that surrounded Chaco for four hundred years a millennium ago considered this bleak and barren portion of their lands the center of their universe. It was their Garden of Eden, but it was hardly a land of milk and honey. And instead of being thrown out of it, they made pilgrimages to it.

As he slowly crept forward, he noted the late summer vegetation, which was as brown as the sand from which it protruded as it struggled to find life-sustaining moisture. Arroyos that provided instant danger in a downpour languidly broke the otherwise flat terrain. No animal life seemed present, lying low to keep cool and conserve energy for tasks best completed during cooler night hours. As he rounded a curve and drove down a gradual decline, he observed the deep sand piles just ahead across the otherwise hard-packed road.

He shifted into four-wheel drive, thankful that he'd listened to Jonathan and had knobby tires mounted on his truck. There must have been a recent gully washer. The myth of Noah's Ark suddenly flashed into his mind. Anyone caught in an arroyo during a sudden downpour would be in immediate danger. It seemed a good metaphor for life.

Even though he was still a couple of miles out from Fajada Butte, the immensity of the imposing outcropping began to overpower him, and he pulled to a stop at the side of the road to get out and take in the vista unimpeded by a cloudy, bug-splattered windshield. No sound broke the desert stillness, and the dust cloud that had been ahead of him was now far enough out that it didn't mar his view.

As he leaned against his truck, he pondered what to believe. His faith had been under assault for years as something in the cosmos pushed and prodded him to move. Yet he hung on, clinging to a belief system he was increasingly finding had no substance or solidity other than tradition. He'd learned it from his mother, who had learned it from hers. There was so much to sort out and pitfalls to avoid, like the victim trap. He would resist that with all his soul.

Jonathan had been right all along: Duality was the source of judgments about good and evil. But in this place where he had come to a momentary stop, the ancients hadn't wasted time and energy on such absurdities. There was no heaven or hell, just life. He surveyed the expanse of the Chacoan valley. This was where they'd put it all together: the cycles of the sun and moon, all in harmony and all one, with no separation. And all in tribute to a god unknown. Or gods unknown. He realized he had much to learn.

He got back in his truck, fired up the engine, and drove on to his destiny.

After arriving at their site in the Chaco campground, Daniel and Jonathan went about the tasks of setting up camp. Daniel stacked the firewood Jonathan had brought next to the grate as Jonathan set the cooler, camping bins, and camp stove on the table. Together they unfolded camp chairs and cots, spreading their bags atop them so they could fall asleep under the star-pocked sky and awaken to the stirrings of the new day in the predawn.

"I love it," Daniel said as he went about his task. "To just be here, sit here, lie here, and look up at the universe. It's a whole new experience. I'm feeling infinitely small in the face of its grandness."

Jonathan pointed to the mesa upon which the sun was resting. "I've always loved gazing up at that. It's so quiet, so beautiful."

Just then a soft melody emanated from one of the shelters the ancients had constructed at the base of the mesa. They turned their attention to the sound and saw a shirtless young man sitting cross-legged with his guitar, his long brown hair pulled back in a ponytail and his face rapturous. Across from him, a young woman with braided black hair flowing along the length of her spine sat with a flute ready to raise to her lips. At a precise moment, she blew into the instrument and the canyon was filled with music sacred in tone.

Daniel turned to look at Jonathan just as Jonathan turned to him, and they locked eyes. "My God," Daniel said. "We've entered another world."

Jonathan nodded, and Daniel realized that even though Jonathan had made many trips to this place, he probably still experienced each time as if it were his first time there. It was always a new day and a new beginning for Jonathan. He was unjaded.

Jonathan began building a small fire as Daniel fired up the camp stove and boiled water for their evening tea. After Jonathan laid out fruit and vegetable slices, bread, and cheese, they filled their plates and settled into their camp chairs to savor the repast accompanied by the gentle guitar and flute concert.

"In ancient Greece," Jonathan said, "this would've been an epicurean feast, but the meal would've been eaten to the strains of a flute and lyre instead of a guitar and flute. The Epicureans understood the profound power of dining to music. But it's deeper. Sound is an energetic vibration. From what I understand, those completely deaf hear sound by feeling it."

Daniel sat in silence, as if moved to another realm by both the music and the place itself. To speak would have felt sacrilegious. The only sounds besides the music came from vehicles slowly grinding their way to their camp spots and the light chatter and clatter of campers setting up their homes for the night. The evening was drawing on. It would be a moonless night, which would allow the stars to appear more brightly. Neither spoke until dusk.

"All I can say is wow," Daniel said as he tilted his head back and took in the vast overhead array. "I don't believe I have ever seen so many stars so clearly. And it's not totally dark yet. You can even make out the constellations."

"It's very difficult to find a place to stargaze that isn't hindered by light pollution," Jonathan said. "Even here, the light pollution from Albuquerque is subtly beginning to intrude. I remember my mother telling us stories about our people in the old country. They were powerful stories. I'm not sure, though, if it's possible for us to fully understand or grasp how people who were largely shepherds and farmers felt. It's become obvious to me that their world was very different from the one in which we live, in countless ways. But even though they and the indigenous people of this land were separated by an ocean and thousands of miles, and even though they developed very different cultures due to their environments and technologies, they shared an understanding of something important."

"How so?"

Jonathan cleared his throat. "Well, like I said, it's becoming very difficult to find places where you can see the stars like this. For my ancestors in Slovakia, even though star-filled night skies were normal, they didn't take what they saw for granted. The night sky was as important to them as the sun in the day. Maybe more so."

Daniel was enthralled by what his ex-partner was expounding on and turned from teacher to student. He leaned back in his camp chair and gazed up at the heavens again. After a few moments, Jonathan continued.

"Today, much of this is intellectual, something we observe and refer to as cool or interesting. But for the ancients, this was a portal leading away from the mundane, everyday reality. It was their way of connecting to and crossing into the spirit world. During the day, they were busy doing all the stuff they needed to do to survive. But at night, they could sit and wonder. And they told stories.

"During the summer evenings, we would sit on our front porch and Mother would tell us stories of our people she learned from her mother, my *bubba*, who escaped the repressive serfdom along with my grandfather, my *dzeda,* in the late nineteenth century. It was magical. Somehow, during the tough times, our hunger and the fear we felt after our dad died all went away when she spoke. She just made us feel better, not only about our conditions then, but about ourselves. Her stories, our stories, gave us dignity." He turned to Daniel. "Today I suppose you can call it validating us."

Daniel smiled. "You know, Jonathan, you just told me more about yourself than you ever have before."

Jonathan's eyes widened and then narrowed in on Daniel. "I have?"

"Yes, you have. You have an engaging way with words when you speak your soul. I believe that when you speak, people will listen. Do you know why?"

Jonathan shook his head.

"Because you're an engaging storyteller. It's something I couldn't quite put my finger on until now, but over the past couple of years, it has been subtly surfacing in you. You've dropped your teacher voice. When you speak now, it's not to inform, instruct, or lecture. It's to tell a story or expound on some philosophical or spiritual point without lecturing or preaching. And that's a huge difference."

Daniel sat back in his chair. "We both taught literature, but you know this better than me. Stories can be more profound and insightful than any philosophical treatise because they're real, even if the story is a tale or myth. And you are real. There's a wondrous softness to your character, an innocence, despite the fact that you've gone through difficult challenges. I never knew your mother, but I suspect you're like her and your grandmother. While you've been toughened, you've not become hardened or coarsened. You still find beauty and magic around you. Just like your people. It's their stories from the hills of Slovakia to the steel mills of Braddock, Pennsylvania, you shared with me. When things get tough and scary, stories are what help people get through it.

"Jonathan, I'm in no position to tell anyone how to live their life, nor do I have the right to, but something just dawned on me. I think you should become a professional writer."

Jonathan looked shocked. "Me? Write a book? I taught books. I never thought to write one. I wouldn't know where to begin or what to write about."

"You're a lifelong learner, and in many ways, you're self-taught. You'd develop your skills relatively quickly. I imagine the first step is to sit down and start writing. As for what to write about, write about your life. You have quite a tale to tell. Tell it. Tell our story. You know, we haven't exactly followed norms or tradition. We didn't take the road less traveled, we've blazed our own trail. And now, as our paths diverge and we go separate ways, you'll have more to tell. Jonathan, no one wants to read about the ordinary. They want to read about the extraordinary, and if our lives over the past three decades aren't considered extraordinary, I don't know what the hell would be."

Jonathan said nothing as he looked up at the heavens. Daniel followed suit. After several minutes, Daniel stood. "I need to relieve myself, and then I'll be turning in. I'm pretty exhausted." He put a hand on Jonathan's shoulder as he passed him. "It's been a day."

When he returned, Jonathan was atop his cot, wrapped in his sleeping bag, stargazing. Daniel climbed into his own sleeping bag and took in the vast array of twinkling stars in the completely black sky that blanketed the canyon. After a few minutes, he could hear Jonathan's gentle snoring and took note of its rhythm. There was symmetry to it all, he decided.

He closed his eyes and pictured Jonathan standing at the top of a mountain with his arms extended going through his seven-direction ritual in which he connected the energies of the seven chakras to the four directions, the sky, and the earth, and finally to the universe. Opening his eyes again, he refocused his attention on the overhead panoply and whispered a prayer before closing them and allowing his breath to come into harmony with Jonathan's.

23

AFTER A BREAKFAST of granola with blueberries, bananas, and green tea in the barely breaking dawn light, they climbed into Jonathan's truck and drove into the park. Shortly past the entry gate, a herd of elk stood a short distance away eyeing them with the same level of curiosity a human would have watching the arrival of the same postal carrier who'd delivered their mail for the past ten years. They drove slowly to take in all the canyon had to offer, and when they reached Pueblo Bonito, Jonathan pulled into the parking area.

"I know you saw this the time you came with me, but I thought you'd want to see it again and learn more about it. In Catholic terms, this was their cathedral. We'll come back later and take the guided tour. It's well worth it."

They drove on until they reached the short turnoff to the Kin Kletso parking area. Jonathan pointed to the top of the mesa. "That's where we'll climb and walk to do our practice. It's best to do it at first light because the morning energies are the most powerful, and it's before most day hikers and sightseers climb up."

Jonathan pulled off his boots and tied them to the back of his daypack. He slipped on what he called his spiritual moccasins, the soft footwear he wore when he worked in his garden. They strapped on their daypacks, grabbed their walking sticks, and hiked the short distance to the Kin Kletso ruins. After circling Kin Kletso with Jonathan pointing out aspects of its architecture, Jonathan pointed up to what looked like a makeshift trail through a steep boulder field. "We climb up through there, and right as you get to the point where you think you hit the wall, you'll see a crevice where the formation separated from the main part of the mass millions of years ago. It's a fun climb. Not treacherous really. Then you come out onto the mesa. It's an incredible view."

Daniel beamed. "I'm game."

After making the climb through the rock crevice above Kin Kletso, Daniel and Jonathan stood, silently taking in the expanse. Stillness blanketed the mesa. The rising sun's rays, filtered by high cirrus clouds, painted the sandstone and granite mesa floor with a pronounced golden hue.

"This is breathtaking," Daniel said.

"Yeah," Jonathan replied with a smile. "And more to come."

Jonathan led the way, pointing out the cairns that marked the path on the uneven, weatherworn, rock-solid ground. They paused at the Stone Circle, which had been chiseled out of the rock by the ancients with rudimentary tools.

"It boggles the mind to think we're walking on a formation created tens of millions of years ago that has been pretty much the same for over a thousand years," Daniel said. "We think of people from then, just over a millennium ago, as ancient, yet when we put them and us within the context of the age of Earth, we're blips in time."

"Yeah," Jonathan replied. "Kind of like nanoseconds. It makes me wonder about the significance of our existence." He stretched out an arm and swept it across the expanse. "Which makes our woes and troubles pale in comparison to the profoundness of all this."

Daniel nodded. "I suppose it's the starkness a place like this presents that makes us reflect on our relationship to the vastness of time and to the eternal. Perhaps it's because Chaco is relatively hostile to life. Unlike the Judeo-Christian myth of Eden, they chose this area as their center. Sort of opposing perspectives. And to think millions of years before people arrived, this was a lush environment teeming with life. This reminds me of the Painted Desert, where it took millions of years for layers of sediment of different colors to build up and erode. And the Petrified Forest, where the rocks once were living trees."

"It's profound to consider, but I like to think that if it weren't for us humans to observe all this, it would be meaningless. It's important to keep in mind that meaning is a human construct. We give all things meaning. Nothing in itself has meaning, which means nothing doesn't mean anything."

Daniel glanced over at him with a raised eyebrow as they walked on. "You're losing me."

Jonathan chuckled. "Me too. I'm chasing myself down my own rabbit hole."

They both laughed and continued walking. Other than an occasional comment about a point of interest, they walked quietly. When Pueblo Alto came into view, Jonathan pointed to it and described the terrain but said he wanted to hike to the overlook before exploring it.

At the edge of the mesa, Jonathan pointed northward. "Can you make out the contour of the road the ancients followed on their pilgrimage? It can be hard to see, but it's there."

"I do. At least I think I do. I'd like to hike it sometime."

"It would be pretty rough, and it's likely on private land now. But I recall Emerson pointing out that no one owns the landscape. So here we stand."

As they took in the vista, Daniel slipped his arm around Jonathan's waist, and in return, Jonathan slipped his around Daniel's and leaned into him. After a bit, they turned and climbed to the remains of the ancient structure of Pueblo Alto. They stood for a minute as Daniel scanned the area, tracing the contour and shape of what had likely been the foundation of a building. As they hiked along the perimeter, Jonathan pointed to the pottery shards strewn across the terrain.

"This is where they practiced their sacred rituals. They would bring their most valued and beautiful pots and smash them on the ground. The reason, it is thought, is that by breaking them, they made them unusable in this world. It was a sacrificial offering."

"Kind of like how the Hebrews killed and sacrificed a lamb," Daniel said.

"Yeah, I suppose," Jonathan replied after a moment. "Except in this case, no life was taken."

On the opposite side of the site, Jonathan pointed to a stone circle. "That was likely a kiva. Looks like a good spot for us to sit and talk. Most apropos."

They carried their daypacks to it and prepared comfortable sitting places. Jonathan spread his jacket on the ground and sat cross-legged in half lotus fashion. Daniel settled into his spot, pushing himself up against his pack for support with his legs bent at the knee and feet planted into the ground.

"I'm afraid sitting meditation style isn't easy for me," he said. "Maybe because I got used to kneeling."

Jonathan smiled. "It takes practice. It took me years to retrain my legs from kneeling and genuflecting to crossing them like this."

Jonathan sighed and was quiet, save for barely audibly chanting, "*Oṃ maṇi padṃe hūṃ*," and Daniel took advantage of his friend's meditation to gather his thoughts. He searched his mind for the right words to tell Jonathan about his decision to leave the priesthood. He'd attempted to find the words several times, but each attempt had failed. This time, he needed to tap in to what was true and real within him and speak from his heart. Jonathan needed and deserved to know.

After several minutes, Jonathan raised his eyes and looked up toward the thin clouds that filtered the sun's rays and then lowered his gaze and looked into Daniel's eyes and bowed. Daniel interpreted that as Jonathan's cue that he was ready.

"Jonathan, you've been there for me since the day we met on that whale boat. And here you are again, even after hearing that I needed to separate from our relationship. I must confess,

I'm still in awe about how you've been handling it. You aren't bitter or angry, nor have you become callous or cold-hearted. I'm not sure if I could be as forgiving or able to detach as you."

Jonathan smiled softly. "Even Buddhists like me have feelings. But we also recognize that the feelings are not us. We understand that it's up to us to decide whether they will control us or we will control them."

Daniel sat reflecting.

After a few moments, Jonathan stretched out his legs, drank from his water bottle, and sat with his knees pulled up and his arms wrapped around them. "Daniel," he said, startling Daniel out of his thoughts, "come on. You're killing yourself trying to find the right words to tell me something. It's time to drop the other shoe. So quit beating yourself up and come out with it. Just say it."

Daniel looked up at him and took a deep breath. "I've resigned from the priesthood. In a short time, I will no longer be a Jesuit."

"I see," Jonathan replied.

"When I told you about leaving our relationship, leaving the priesthood was something I was pondering, but I hadn't made a final decision then. And I was afraid to tell you for fear that you'd try to talk me *out of* ending our partnership and *into* formalizing our relationship."

Jonathan nodded. "I see."

After a few moments of quiet, Daniel shook his head. "You're not making this easy for me."

"Should I?"

"No, of course not. But I think I'd be able to handle this better if you'd rant and rave. But that's not you, and I know you're not playing the wounded martyr."

"No, I'm not. You know how much I despise self-pity. So no, I'm not. But as I said, even Buddhists have feelings. You've given me much to process, Daniel. It will take time for me to do that." He paused and cocked his head to one side. "I have one question," he said at last. "Why didn't you share any of this with me when it began to surface?"

"Because I had to figure it out on my own. And you were one of the two life-loves I came to realize I would need to part with."

"And the other?"

"The priesthood, of course. As a priest, I was married to the Church, as I was to you—her religiously; you spiritually."

Daniel moved closer to Jonathan, knelt back on his haunches, and took Jonathan's hands in his. "Jonathan, you've been my one true personal love, and I suspect that will never change. But so much has been coming at me over the past few months, my head feels like a whirling dervish. The only one I opened up to was Vincente, and that was only recently. And now I'm in therapy with Sophia, his wife."

Jonathan smiled softly again. "I know."

"You know? How?"

"Well, I didn't know about you seeing Sophia professionally, but I did meet her. And since we're being totally open, I'll tell you that I asked Vincente to help me sort out what was going on with you. He and I met at the Bodhi Mandi Zen Center, and on my way back, I went through Taos and met Sophia."

Daniel felt Jonathan tighten his hands around his own, and then he was pulled toward his longtime partner.

"As you can see," Jonathan said, "while I didn't know the specifics of what exactly was happening, I knew you, and I still do. What you're telling me is really clarifying what I was sensing underneath but couldn't put my finger on. I admit, my love, this is disconcerting for me, but I have to say, you're showing incredible courage." Jonathan eased his grip, and both sat back on their haunches. "Daniel, I want the best for you, but I wonder if you've considered the financial ramifications of your decision. After all, you will no longer have a steady source of income and free room and board."

"I have, and to be honest, something related happened that made my decision easier. Do you remember my Aunt Lucille, the aunt I told you I was very close to?"

Jonathan nodded.

"A couple of months ago, she called and asked how I was doing. As we talked, she sensed that I was struggling. I could never keep anything from her, so when she pressed me, I gave her a rundown on what was getting me down. A week later, she called back and said she'd set up a trust fund for me if I decided to leave the priesthood. But only if. She made that stipulation clear because in no way did she want her money getting into the hands of the Church. So between the money I've managed to save and Aunt Lucille's generosity, I'll be fine until I get settled and decide on a future pursuit."

"I'm very happy for you. The Fates are working overtime for you. Everything seems to be falling into place."

A look of consternation crossed Jonathan's face, and Daniel asked what was wrong.

"I felt a chill overtake me," Jonathan replied as he closed his eyes. After a few moments, he opened them. "Daniel, as I said, you're making a very courageous decision. But I'm worried."

"Why?"

"I don't think you understand the hell you've signed up for."

"Jonathan, I don't believe I'll be going to hell because I've left the priesthood."

"That's not what I'm talking about. I'm talking about the hell that will descend on you because of your decision. Albert Camus said that the reason the Church dealt with heretics so harshly was because she decided there were no worse enemies than errant children. It's the reason my brother was so brutal toward me."

"But I'm not a heretic. I haven't left the Church, just renounced my vows."

"True, but you're damn close to being one. You won't be just another priest who has walked away. You're gay and will most certainly pursue that aspect of your life, whether with me or another man. Some from the outside might try to play on that and turn you into a cause célèbre. And if that happens, and I think it highly likely, the powers that be will throw all they can against you. And as courageous and strong as you are, I'm not sure you'll have the mettle to withstand or handle the incoming tribulation."

"You did, and your brother forgave you at the end."

"Did he, or was it only my hopeful interpretation of his last gesture? And look at the toll it took on me. I almost didn't make it. Besides, I wasn't a priest. In the eyes of the Church, I was just some shmuck schoolteacher. Daniel, you and I are tough and strong in different ways. I'm like my mother; you're like your father. My strength is more feminine in nature. It comes from deep inside. It comes from a steely steadfastness of the mind. Yours is more masculine. It arises from passion, from your heart and sometimes from your ego. Daniel, I want to be wrong about this. I want you to be able to withstand the buffeting blows of the storm I believe will head your way. But to do that, I truly believe you will need to develop a toughness, a thick alligator hide like you've never had."

Daniel dropped his eyes and stared at the ground but didn't see it. The brutal truth of what Jonathan was saying stunned him and swirled in his mind. He wanted to retort, but he had no comeback, no defense. It was true. The one thing he never could stand being accused of was being weak. And when he was attacked, he lashed out. And here was Jonathan telling him exactly that. He looked back up into Jonathan's compassionate eyes and nodded.

Jonathan pushed himself up in a standing position, reached down, and grabbed Daniel's wrist, pulling him up. He lifted his daypack and strapped it over his shoulders. Daniel did likewise.

"Daniel, I know what I just said wasn't pleasant to hear, but it's critical that you move forward with no illusions. The Church hasn't survived as the most powerful and lucrative institution in human history by being gracious and forgiving when it comes to those who break away from its fold. No, you won't be burned at the stake. At least not literally. But the fire could get hot."

Daniel put a half smile on his face. "As I told you last night, you do have a way with words—use of hyperbole without being hyperbolic being one of them. But I hear you. The road ahead will be rough as all less traveled ones are, but I'm ready. I hope. I'll toughen up like you have or I'll crash and burn. But don't put foolish money on the latter happening."

"Good man," Jonathan replied, tapping him on the shoulder. "Onward, not-so-Christian soldier." He turned toward the trail. "C'mon. Let's start down. I'd like to hike out to Peñasco Blanco and have lunch before it gets too warm. We can do the tour of Pueblo Bonito this afternoon."

Jonathan pointed ahead to the south to another site as they hiked. "That's Tsin Kletzin way across that other mesa. Its name comes from the Navajo for charcoal place because of the charred wood found there. It's a very powerful sight to look back from there at Pueblo Alto. So much to learn."

"Yeah, and for me not only about Chaco." He paused and then said, "Thank you, Jonathan, for the strong words. I trust you to be brutally honest with me. Vincente, James, and Richard can talk to me that way, but you have an incisive manner to cut through the bullshit. In the end, you're the only one I could never con."

Jonathan stopped and turned toward Daniel. "One more thing before we drop the discussion. Know that I still need you. You're my other half. But that's something we'll figure out as time goes on."

Daniel nodded, and Jonathan turned and led the way back down the trail.

"So where to after we leave here?" Jonathan asked as they hiked.

"I'm not totally sure, though from here, I plan to head south and pick up the interstate at Thoreau and head toward the coast."

"Hmm, going through Thoreau."

Daniel chuckled. "I know what you're thinking. The symbolism of Thoreau the town, and Thoreau the philosopher. My copy of *Walden* is back in Denver. I'll grab another at a bookstore along the way."

"Fantastic idea. Pretty good companion to travel with as you begin your life anew."

"Agreed. Along with Jack Kerouac. I'll snag a copy of *On the Road* too. Maybe I can try doing an imitation of Dean Moriarty." He paused. "But then, on second thought, maybe not."

ACKNOWLEDGMENTS

With humble gratitude, I thank first and foremost the friends and readers who encouraged me to write a follow-up story, perhaps a sequel, to *Sisyphus Wins*. Their promptings and probing questions helped me decide on the focus of the story and the development of Daniel, the main character. My deepest appreciation to my beta readers—Joe Holub, Marcia Holub, Steven Craig, Barb Lundy, Donna Taylor, and John Taylor—for their invaluable contributions, insights, and suggestions for improving my first draft. And many thanks to those who have read and endorsed *The Lion's Den*.

A special tribute to my editor extraordinaire, Melanie Mulhall, not only for her stellar work on improving the text—making my words sing and dance more harmoniously—but also for her guidance and for sharing her wisdom and sagacity on the psychological, philosophical, and spiritual elements in the story. A big-time tip of the hat to Nick Zelinger for creating the masterful cover scene and for laying out the interior of the book and another to Veronica Yager for her tech support, particularly with regard to my website and e-book developments.

Finally, I thank the muses and other ethereal spirits and energies who inspired and guided me throughout the writing process. For it is from the well of the unconscious that this story sprang.

About the Author

Jerry Fabyanic is the award-winning author of the novel *Sisyphus Wins and of Food for Thought: Essays on Mind and Spirit* series. Jerry is an essayist, philosophical explorer and provocateur, and erstwhile teacher of English and social studies who counts Herman Melville, John Steinbeck, Toni Morrison, Carl Jung, and Joseph Campbell among the thinkers who have influenced him most.

Jerry lives in the historical mining town of Georgetown in Clear Creek County, Colorado, where he explores the symbolic world of myth and story in his writings from atop his aerie. As the years pass, Jerry's love affair with the Colorado Rocky Mountains grows deeper. He has climbed thirty-four of Colorado's fourteeners, has run seven marathons, and still carves the bumps through the powder and timber of Mary Jane's Eagle Wind territory.

Jerry has learned the importance of being mindful. His daily practice is to pay attention to guideposts, junctures that initially seem coincidental but prove to be path-altering experiences. Whether running at 8,500 feet, skiing moguls, or reaching for an outcropping at 13,000 feet, Jerry reminds himself of his place and role as a denizen of Mother Earth.

You can read more about Jerry and his works at *www.jerryfabyanic.com.*